Under the Pear Tree

Bernadette Conte

UNDER THE PEAR TREE
THE HEART OF CARDI'S YARD

Capotosto, Cardi, Messori, Palumbo, Ruggieri, and Vellucci tenants. Singing and dancing to Papa's music, under the pear tree with friends and family. Uncle Rico Cardi sitting in his black Cadillac and Marietta Palumbo watching.

MEMORIES ARE FOREVER

Papa playing the guitar

*Zia Maria Civita and Zio Luigino Sinapi
with Capotosto children*

Mary Palumbo and Madeline Velluci dancing

This book was printed in the United States of America.

Date: July 21, 2020

Books by author: Eviva Maria, Madonna della Civita

Amazon. Com, Barnes and Noble, Xlibris Publishing

To order additional copies of books, contact Amazon.com
Bernadette Conte
   contessabc@verizon.net
   401-942-4127

TABLE OF CONTENTS

DEDICATION

With deepest gratitude:

To those who made it possible for my generation and future generations to keep our heritage alive. They profoundly touched my life.

My spiritual mother, Our Lady of Lourdes and Maria Santissima della Civita, the mother of our Lord and Savior Jesus Christ, God of our ancestors. I give it all to her for inspiring my life. In turn, she gives all to her Son, Jesus and provides for us. "Totus Tuus."

Our families and future generations, that they will remember and cherish their profound family heritage.

My children, Katherine Maria Conte and Ralph Charles Conte, Jr., my greatest loves and gifts from above, for their continual support, wisdom, and love. They both lived in Italy for several years and spent much cherished time with relatives in Rome, Itri, Caserta, and Fondi.

Ralph, who continually tells me to live life and do what makes me happy. Each day, he asks me, "Ma, what are your plans for today? The clock is ticking."

Katherine, who has been my guiding light throughout her adult life, especially when I feel stuck and have difficulty moving forward. She has prompted me to listen to that voice within, and to follow it.

My cherished, loving, grandchildren, Zoë, Raphael, Kali, Krishan, and my great-grandson, Leo Matthew Jr., who continue to inspire me and are the loves of my life.

In Memory Of

My parents, Caterina (Gaetanina) Cardi and Cosmo Capotosto.

My husband, Raffaele Gerardo (Ralph Charles) Conte.

Our family members and ancestors, especially our grandparents, whose realities are the basis for these stories.

Our great-grandparents, Gaetana and Alfonso Cardi who loved, cared for, and provided a home for their grandchild, Gaetanina.

Gaetanina as a teenager

Caterina (Gaetanina) Cardi and Cosmo Capotosto

Bisnonna Gaetana and Bisnonno Alfonso Cardi

ACKNOWLEDGEMENTS

My mother, Caterina (Gaetanina) Cardi Capotosto, had more courage and love within her than I've ever known in any other human being. Her deep faith in God and love for everyone was a witness to her intense spiritual life. Her never-ending sacrifices will always be remembered and honored. Throughout her life, she urged me to "scrivi e recorda" (write and remember) the stories she told me. I do not know the history of her brothers and sisters or their lives in America as children. I can only write from my mother's memory and perspective from the life she shared with her grandparents, Gaetana and Alfonso Cardi, and her cousin, Reverend Amedeo (Roland) Cardi. Gaetanina and Roland were raised by their grandparents and had a great love and respect for one another throughout their lives. Their knowledge is that of a living experience with our ancestors.

Cosmo Capotosto (Papa), whose talents were endless. He taught our entire family a great deal. Although he didn't live long enough to know his grandchildren and great-grandchildren, he will live on in our stories of him. Even though we did not know our grandparents, Benedetta and Onorato, Papa made sure we knew them through him.

My late husband. Raffaele C. Conte, who encouraged and supported many of my endeavors, especially to research our religious and family roots. He always welcomed and encouraged entertaining relatives, friends, or visitors from other states, and countries, especially Italy.

Gaetana Pernarella Cardi (Bisnonna) and Alfonso Cardi (Bisnonno) were our great-grandparents. I know Gaetana and Alfonso through their grandchild, Gaetanina, whom they raised as if she were their child. It is because of their faith and heroic efforts that Gaetanina's childhood blindness was healed. I know them because Gaetanina never stopped talking about them and her parents, Maria Civita and Antonio Cardi.

Loreta Cardi, (spouse of Ascanio Cardi and Enrico Cardi's mother), provided the court documentation and inventory records for the estate of Gaetana Cardi. Reverend Amedeo Cardi (Roland), who gave us the written history of our family origins and the explanation of our Cardi family coat of arms. He and Gaetanina gave to us the family names of our ancestors, dating back to Domenico, father of Bisnonno Alfonso so that our original family tree could be constructed by Patricia Paolella. Roland will always be remembered with great love and respect.

A special thanks and gratitude to:

Enrico Cardi for documents and information that he provided for me, and for the kindness and hospitality he and Tina showed to my family and me.

Paola Sepe Cardi and Gianpaolo Cardi, who were always caring, welcoming, and provided for my traveling needs in Itri. Gianpaolo and Paola welcomed visitors from our family with open arms. Paola gave me a copy of *Tra Sacro e Profano in Terra d'Itri*, a book written by her author cousin Pino Pecchia, which she translated from Italian into English. His work provided the information I needed regarding the history of the *Civita*. Pino gave me written authorization for the publication of his biographical notes for my book, "Eviva Maria, Madonna della Civita." In turn, I gave to him a copy of Don Michele Manzi's renowned, *Discorso*.

Alfonso Di Biase who provided help with transportation, photographing documents in Itri and for the friendship and love I experienced from him. Dr. Vincenzo and Fortunata Di Biase for their hospitality.

Dr. Ettore Cardi, for his hospitality at his home in Rome, and allowing access to his home and family albums in Itri.

Cavaliere (Zio) Pasquale Cardi, Cosmo Cardi, Carolina Cardi, Paolo and Filomena Di Biase, Vincenza Cardi, Ascanio Cardi and Maria

Rosaria Pesce Cardi, Lidia Cardi, Olinda Manzi Cardi, Rita Patrizia Pirelli, Sergio, Ilda, Nicolina, and Zio Vincenzo Capotosto.

The Contes who reside in Fondi, for their hospitality. They own the largest wholesale fruit and produce company in southern Italy.

In gratitude to:

Caroline Curelli, whose artistic genius photoshopped the original photo for the book cover. Through her talent, I was able to obtain a photo of my father playing the guitar.

Matthew Morse, for his tremendous talent in designing the book cover.

Katherine Boden, MLIS from the Cranston Library, for her patience and technical support.

Rosalba Martini Belfiore from Rome, for her friendship, hospitality, and the transportation she provided for me throughout Rome, and Fondi, and who patiently translated documents from Italian into English. Her creative talents were beyond my expectation.

Professor Candice Simmons, for her friendship, advice, and editing, and for her untiring efforts and skills for the completion of this book.

Ettore Cardi's book: *Una Notte del 1943 Nella Campagna di Itri*

Photos:

Ancestry
Boston Globe
Mary Barone
Roland Barone
Cranston Historical Society
Cranston City Hall
Luke Capotosto
Donna Cardi
Enrico Cardi
Ettore Cardi
Ron Cardi
Angela Capotosto Cardillo
Reverend Angelo Caruso
Catholicism Pure and Simple
Ron Cece
Cindy Conti
Maryann Ferri Crudale
Department of Naturalized Citizen; My Heritage
Jeanette Palumbo D'Amico
Alfonso Di Biase
Roberta Di Fusco Di Marco
Donna Longo Di Michele
Ellis Island Records
Dolly Haibon
Peggy Healy
Audrey Crudale Hoyos
Karen Crudale Kuski
Maria LaTour Kadison
La Provincia
Stephanie LaTour
Donald Migliori
Michael Migliori
Stephen Migliori

New American Bible
Debra Izzo Ostrowski
Antonio Palotta
Arthur Palotta
Maryann Sinapi Peterson
Providence Historical Society
Providence Journal
The Evening Bulletin
Marie Capotosto Vartanian
World War II archives

"Sometimes the strongest among us are the ones who smile through the pain, cry alone, and fight battles no one knows about."

Gaetanina and Bernadette

INTRODUCTION
SCRIVI E RICORDA
(WRITE AND REMEMBER)

At the request of my daughter, Katherine Maria Conte, I began writing a cookbook of family recipes. As I continued writing about my mother, father, and family members, family history kept cropping up. I then knew I must keep the promise I had made to my mother, to write and remember what she had told me.

Since my early teens, I collected historical documents and wrote and saved notes from conversations with Mama. She would talk to me for hours and hours about her life in Itri, Italy. She would say to me, "Benedetta, scrivi e ricorda," I feel compelled to write and to fulfill Caterina (Gaetanina) Cardi Capotosto's wish to share with our family what she told me.

I can only write what I experienced, discovered, and was told. I can only tell what was told to me by my mother and Cardi relatives who lived in Italy. We were six children, and each of us has our own unique story.

I want to pass on the shared history I was given when I was a young girl and throughout my adult life, to my children, grandchildren, great-grandchildren, nieces, nephews, and cousins, in the hope that they will remember Mama, Papa, and our relatives and ancestors. My purpose is to share the love and traditions that I was taught and the love that our family always had for one another, the love that Mama had for her children, their spouses, grandchildren, and her great-grandchildren. Mama loved the world and everyone in it. Papa, who lived until the age of 56, never lived long enough to know the love that would have been in store for him from his grandchildren and great-grandchildren.

Cardi Coat of Arms

CHAPTER 1
EXPLANATION OF THE CARDI EMBLEM

Written by Reverend Roland Cardi

The name Cardi is derived from a plant of the same name, which is common in Italy and grows wild in the fields. The plant at full growth is about two feet high. It is all covered and protected by small, but sharp thorns that sting if you touch them. Thus, saying, "We sting like the cardi."

In the family emblem, is a helmet with two leaves at its sides standing on the Scutum or escutcheon. In the middle of the Scutum, there is a column supporting three flowers of cardi, whence we take our name, and surrounded by three tongues of flames on each side and below. A ribbon goes around the column and ties two branches, one of the olives at the left, and one of the laurels at the right. Two stars shine in the upper part.

3

The Noble Origin of the Cardi Family

The emblem indicates that our family has a noble origin and indeed our ancestors had the title of Conti. In the church of the Annunziata in Itri, where our family originates, under the big painting representing the Annunciation suspended in the chorus, it is written that a Joseph Cardi rebuilt that church e comitatus Cardi (from the Count's Cardi). The same thing is repeated on a marble inscription placed on the right side of the main nave, commemorating that event that took place in the 18th century. We do not know when they ceased using that title. Maybe a large number of new families caused the division of the properties and the lack of substantial wealth necessary to sustain the title.

Our family originates from Corsica (Greece). During the Middle Ages, when the Turks were a powerful nation, they used to make incursions on the shores of Italy to pillage valuable things and to plunder the people. To meet those pirates and to spy on their coming, the Popes and other Princes of Italy built towers along the shores of the Mediterranean Sea.

Every tower contained a small number of soldiers. A Cardi, who came from Corsica, was the head of a group of these watching posts. He established himself at Itri and there his family remained.

Our relative, Zio Antonio Cardi of Itri, who possesses a history book of our family, used to tell me that even in the past century, at the time of Garibaldi, the Cardi family was a wealthy one. He told me this story: A certain Don Leone Cardi filled with admiration for King Victor Emanuel II, Garibaldi, and Cavour, and with hatred against the church, as was the custom of those very troublesome times. Instead of calling the priest, he blessed it himself in the name of Garibaldi, Victor Emanuel, and Cavour. He started the fire, but a few days later everything fell apart, with the laughter of all the town.

The father of Zio Titto, who died poor in our house, was the owner of the two palaces near the fountain at Itri. He sold everything to finance Garibaldi's expedition to Sicily and left his children in misery.

The Cardi family owned a large estate from the present fountain, which is still our property, to the country called St. Mark. Their palace is located on the Via Appia. This house is divided into two parts: one half has been sold to Benedetto Soscia, alias Tittarielle, and the other half has been bought by our relative, Teodoro Cardi. Cardinal Ippolito D'Este died in that house. In the 15th century, he was the protector of the great poet Ludovico Ariosto.

Our Immediate Ancestors

Our immediate ancestors came from Itri a town of about 10,600 people located between Naples and Roma, on the ancient Via Appia. It is 91.6 miles south of Rome.

Our grandfather, Alfonso Cardi, was the son of Domenico Cardi and Maria Civita Agresti. Domenico's father was Antonio Cardi and his mother was Giacinta Simeone. Maria Civita and Domenico had four sons: Alfonso, Felice, Francesco, Gaetano Cardi, and two daughters: Lucia and Giacinta.

Uncle Francesco Cardi was a tall and handsome man. He had two sons and two daughters. One of his sons, Uncle Luigi Cardi, is currently still living in Itri. (Gianpaolo Cardi from Itri is from this lineage). Another uncle, Fiore Cardi, is living in Brooklyn, New York. Gaetano Cardi had a daughter Marietta, who was married to Luigi De Luca-La Nonechella. She was married in New York and has since passed away.

Gaetano's sons are all in Italy. His son, Vincent, died during the First World War. Another son, Carlo Cardi, was married to Nellie Saccoccio (now deceased) of Knightsville, in Cranston, Rhode Island. Zia Giacinta had two sons and two daughters. One son, Alberto, a contractor, is living in Naples, Italy. The other son is Uncle Michele Ialongo of Cranston, Rhode Island. Michele married Frances Saccoccia of Knightsville. Their children are Marie, Giacinta (Joanne), Anna, Lucy, Angela, Domenic, Michael, and Anthony. My sisters, Anna and Marie, are comari with Angela Ialongo Calvey. Giacinta's daughter, Lucy, married Emilio DeLuca of Brooklyn, New York, and Angelina is married to Frank La Rocco of New York.

Zia Lucia had one daughter, who was married to Peppino Ruggieri. They had a grocery store in Itri. Felice Cardi's one son, Pasquale, was a mason in Itri. He now lives in Marseille, France.

Francis and Michael Ialongo family
Photo: Peggy Healy

Reverend Amedeo (Roland) Cardi

CHAPTER 2
OUR FAMILY

Written by Reverend Roland Cardi

Alfonso Cardi, our great-grandfather, Alfonso was tall and good look-ing, sporting a beard and mustache. He always had a smile on his lips and kindness in his heart. He was a hard-working man, attached to his family. Through his work and sacrifices, he succeeded in building six rimesse (garages) with two rooms on the first rimesse. Our rimesse was located on the main road between Naples and Rome.

He married Gaetana Pernarella, from Monte San Biagio, fifteen miles from Itri. Gaetana was a very energetic woman. She had some property as her dowry. When I was a boy (Roland), Gaetanina and I went with Nonna and her relatives to Monte San Biagio, to get grapes from our *vigna* (vine-yard), pears from our big trees, and wheat from the fields. A few years before grandpa died, Gaetana sold everything to build the *rimesse*. She would often say to her family, "Solo sono nata e solo deve morire" (alone was I born, and alone I shall die).

Our grandfather inherited his father's house on Via St. Gerdamo. Of their five children born to him and Gaetana, Maria Civita died, but her siblings, Immacolatina, Antonio, Domenico, Vincenzo, lived in their family home. All of his children except Vincenzo (James) were married from that same house. In the division of the property, the first floor of the house went to Zia Imma-colatina and the other half went to Domenico. In that house, Roland, Irene, Aguila, and Pio were born.

Alfonso and his family had cars and horses. They carried merchandise from Formia or Naples, and before other towns many times during the year. They stayed out a whole week and when they went far, they gave me (Roland) and Gaetanina la bona Mano, a little tip.

Grandfather had a big CART with three horses and a small CART with a horse and donkey. The last and best horse we had was named Marcone. It was an Arabian horse, the pride of the family, the best horse of the town. It was bought by our father, Domenico, in Naples when he was still young. Our father loved that horse. The last donkey was named Cicciollo, a very good one. We used it for many things. We had a two-wheel buggy and Cicciollo pulled it, with us, on to the beach of Vendicio every year. (Vendicio, very close to Itri), was where Gaetanina went with her grandmother and Roland, for summer vacation. He did not like to give back rides, many times he threw me on the ground, but he was a very good worker. I did cry when we sold the donkey. Now its bones are resting in peace.

The family in Itri was composed of Grandpa, Grandma, me, (Roland), Gaetanina, and Zio Titto. Returning from a trip, Grandpa died in Formia in 1919, in the arms of Micelino Mancini alias Forbicetta, our Garzone, or helper, who was with him. He died suddenly. He was buried in Itri. After his death, Grandma continued the trade for a while, but a little later she was compelled to sell everything. We kept only Marcone and Cicciollo. Zio Titto died in the year of the Coronation, 1927.

Grandma died one year later, in October 1928, while I was in the seminary at Naples. (October 15, 1928, according to Gaetanina and documentation). After the funeral, we legally closed the house, waiting for letters from our uncles and fathers. Zia Immacolatina did not like the idea, because she wanted to grab everything; therefore, she made trouble for Gaetanina, who took away her belongings the same night that Grandma died. She accused Gaetanina of stealing things from the house. Gaetanina wanted to go to America to join her family, but she had to stay almost another year until the judge dismissed the case. Even our relatives, Zio Teodoro Cardi (Enrico's father), and Zio Alfredo Cardi had trouble because they were accused of stealing with Gaetanina. We had a hard time on that occasion. But I will always remember the great kindness of Zio Teodoro, who took us into his house when we were left unprotected, while Zia Immacolatina would put us in jail if she could.

Gaetanina married Cosmo Capotosto and soon after, they came to America. I had to wait another year until I was ordained, on July 20, 1930, in Itri. On September 1, I sailed for America to visit my family. We left all our property in the hands of Zio Teodoro as our Administrator.

Estate left of the fountain

The Cardi Oxen

Grandpa Antonio Cardi with other Italian immigrants,
Johnstown, Pennsylvania

"May God endow your hearts with the wisdom to judge His people uprightly, so that the virtues of your ancestors may never fade, and their glory may pass to all of their descendants?"

Ecclesiasticus/Sirach V 45:2
(New American Bible)

Maria Civita Saccoccio Cardi   *Antonio B. Cardi*

CHAPTER 3
GRANDMA MARIA CIVITA AND GRANDPA ANTONIO B. CARDI

Maria Civita Saccoccio, daughter of Costanzo and Angela Lepizzera, married Antonio Abbondio Cardi, elder son of Gaetana Pernarella and Alfonso Cardi, in Itri, Italy.

A census document lists 1899 as the date of Antonio's first arrival in America. Another document indicates that he first arrived at Ellis Island on May 10, 1900. Domenico, Antonio's brother arrived in America on June 16, 1900. After working on the railroad as a foreman for several years, Antonio returned to Itri and arrived back in America on the ship, Roma, in April 1902. Traveling with him was his two-year-old son Alfonso, Maria Civita, and his youngest brother Vincenzo. Antonio went back to Johnstown, Pennsylvania, taking with him his family and his brother Vincenzo. Domenico joined his brother Antonio when he arrived in America. Aunt Angelina, Uncle Alfred, and Dr. Alphonse Cardi were born in Johnstown.

The brothers later settled with many Itrani immigrants in Knightsville, a small town in Cranston, Rhode Island, once known as "Monkey Town." Antonio and Maria Civita purchased tenement houses and three acres of land in Knightsville for $2500.00 on July 24, 1905. Antonio lived with his family on the second floor of his property at 1707 Cranston Street. On January 9, 1914, he purchased lots at 1903 Cranston Street. The A. Cardi Construction Co. garage was located behind the tenement houses. Recently, I learned from our cousin Aguila (Angie) Cardi Cantone's daughters, Rita De Quattro and Irene Martin, that the Domenico Cardi family lived in one of grandfather Antonio's tenement houses until they purchased their own property, at the corner of Cranston and Knight Streets. According to a census document, Domenico was listed as living with Antonio. It seemed several of the immigrant relatives including Michael Ialongo, lived with Antonio when they first arrived in America.

Antonio later built two brick buildings on Cranston Street, home to Marty's Variety Store and the Cranston Social Club.

Uncle Alfred Cardi, a pharmacist, established Medical Arts Pharmacy in the building next door at 1701 Cranston Street. The office of A. Cardi Construction Co., founded by Antonio B. Cardi, occupied the front portion of the second floor. After their marriages, his sons, Alfred, Americo, and their families occupied the large apartment behind the construction office.

The Cardi brothers working on the Pennsylvania Railroad

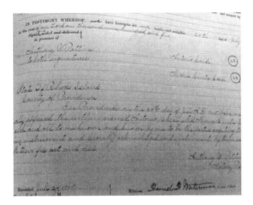

*The Legal purchase agreement for property and land on Cranston Street
(Cranston City Hall)*

Antonio B. Cardi Construction Co.

Census document
(Ancestry)

Alfred Cardi, founder of Medical Arts Pharmacy and owner of
A. Cardi Construction Co.

Americo S. Cardi, founder of Cardi Corp.
And owner of A. Cardi Construction Co.

Antonio B. Cardi, son of Americo
Cardi Corp.

Stephen Cardi, son of Americo
Cardi Corp.

Stephen Cardi (Antonio's son), Cardi Corp.Driving a restored A. Cardi
Construction Co. truck

The Cardi brothers, Antonio, Domenico, and Vincenzo were hard-working and went into various businesses. They independently went into the construction business. Rosa and her family opened a variety and hardware store at the corner of Cranston and Knight Streets. Her sons, Peter and Nicholas later established Cardi's Furniture, in the same building. Vincenzo, Antonio's brother, opened a bakery at 1792 Cranston Street, a wholesale liquor business, a bar in Connecticut, and a construction company. Many years later, when he moved to Arizona, Vincenzo opened a water company and a construction company.

The brothers acquired much property in Knightsville and other parts of Rhode Island. The Cardis believed in acquiring land, as buying land was a great investment for them. Through many trials and hardships, with their undying faith in the Maria Santissima della Civita and through hard work and endurance, the Cardis became prosperous.

Maria Civita and Antonio had six children: Alfonso (spouse, Anna Carrigan), Angelina (spouse, Arthur Crudale), Alfred (spouse, Adeline Perrino), Anna (spouse, Joseph Migliori), Gaetanina (spouse, Cosmo Capotosto), and Americo (spouse, Jeanette Perrino). Alfred and Americo married sisters. Maria Civitina (spouse, William Longo), was the only child of our stepmother, Maria Battista, and Antonio. Aunt Mary (Civitina) was never referred to as a stepsister; she was referred to as "my sister Mary." Mama was the fifth child.

Grandma, Maria Civita was a beautiful, creative woman with many talents. She baked bread to sell to immigrant families in Pennsylvania, in an outdoor brick oven Antonio built for her. Within several years, she and Antonio had saved enough money to acquire land and tenement houses when they moved to Knightsville. When they arrived in Knightsville, Maria Civita opened a store. It isn't clear if she still made and sold bread, as she had done in Pennsylvania.

Working, taking care of six children, and her frequent pregnancies, took a toll on Maria Civita's health. It was unfortunate that she died of a convulsion at the age of 37. Americo (Stefano) was a nine-month-old baby when she died, and my mother, Gaetanina, was beginning her third year of life. It is said that she suffered extreme bleeding, which may have caused the convulsion. Some have stated she had a stroke and was pregnant with another child when she died. Alfonso, Maria Civita's elder son, desperately ran for miles to the doctor's office to get treatment for his mother, but it was too late. No one could help her. I often wonder if that event is what inspired Alfonso to become a doctor.

Antonio faced the dilemma of raising six children, one of whom was his three-year-old, legally blind daughter, Gaetanina. There seemed to be little hope for the child. Daily, her brother Alfonso would carry her on his shoulders and walk miles to the doctor's office for her eyes to be treated. Doctors said there was not much they could do for her. Antonio could not care for his daughter after the death of Maria Civita.

At the urging of his parents, Antonio took four-year-old Gaetanina (Mama) to Italy, in the hope that doctors in Naples would be able to cure her. Antonio's parents put plans in motion for Gaetanina to be seen by specialists at a hospital in Naples, Italy.

Antonio applied for a passport for himself and his infant child on October 22, 1912. There was always a question whether or not Antonio himself took his daughter to Italy. Some have said her father sent his daughter to Italy with his close friends, possibly her godparents, Nuziote and Raffaele Carnevale, but the documents tell a different story. During my research, I found a document from the Department of Naturalized Citizens, 2 Market Square, Providence, Rhode Island, with the name of Antonio Cardi.

It clearly showed that Antonio petitioned for a passport for himself and his infant daughter. The document stated that he would not stay in Italy for more than two years. Giuseppe Lepezzera of 1689 Cranston Street, Cranston, Rhode Island was a witness to this document. This decision by Antonio to go to Italy and to put his children, Alfonso, Alfred, Anna, and Angelina into an orphanage for four months, was shocking and unsettling for the children. Their only consolation was that they were together. The unpleasant memory and trauma of their four months stay at an orphanage, remained with each child throughout their lives

Antonio needed help with 9-month old Americo (Stefano) after his wife's death. He sought the help of two Itrani immigrants who lived in

Knightsville. After the death of his mother, Maria Civita, 9-month old Americo, was breastfed by Maria Civita Maggiacomo and Maria Civita Fargiorgio. It seemed that each child, after the death of their mother, experienced their own deep traumas: the four children placed in the orphanage, the baby who needed his mother's milk and no longer felt her caresses and nurturing, and the 3-year old blind child who was no longer cared for and loved by her mother, Maria Civita. Still grieving the loss of her mother, Gaetanina (Mama) was suddenly taken away from her siblings and brought to people she did not know in a foreign land.

Throughout Mama's life, the rejection, abandonment, longing, and emptiness she felt with the absence of her mother and family, remained deep within her.

Shortly after his return to Itri, Antonio (Grandpa) reconnected with a friend, Maria Battista Figliozzi, of Monte San Biagio, and they were married. He and Maria Battista returned to America without 4-year old Gaetanina. Maria Battista became the mother of Antonio's five children, along with their daughter together, Maria Civitina.

Alfred, Antonio, Angelina (R)
Gaetanina, Americo, Anna (F)

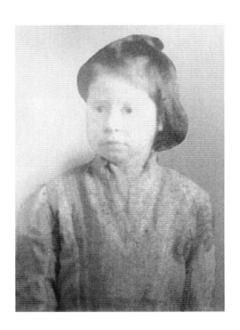

2 year old Gaetanina

Passport for Gaetanina and Antonio
Department of Naturalized Citizens

Americo, Angelina, Anna, Alfonso, Alfred, Maria Battista,
Maria Civitina, Antonio

Grandma Maria Battista and Maria Civitina

30 year old, Dr. Alfonso Blaise Cardi

*Funeral at the Original St. Ann's Church
over 1000 people attend*

Obituary: The Evening Bulletin

Gaetanina's cousins and childhood friends (Enrico's sisters)
Wanda Cardi

Vera Cardi

Amedeo (Roland) Bisnonna Gaetana, Gaetanina

CHAPTER 4
GAETANINA'S LIFE IN ITRI

A ntonio's parents, Gaetana and Alfonso, met the ship carrying Mama and her father on its arrival in Naples. The grandparents immediately took their granddaughter to the best hospital in the city of Naples, to see Dr. Guliano Cardonanno and Dr. Pasquale Ruggieri. Mama was in the hospital for three days, undergoing many tests. Blood clots were found underneath the eyelids. The doctors would not touch her. They emphatically advised her father and grandparents not to have anyone ever touch her eyes. Antonio, his daughter, and his parents returned to Itri. Gaetana and Alfonso did not give up hope. Their faith and trust in God led them in a different direction.

Santina and Annamaria Soprano
Photo: Dolly Haibon

Gaetana took her granddaughter to see Annamaria Soprano, from Itri, who was well-known for her gift of healing eyes. Annamaria was the mother of Benedetto Soprano, and grandmother to Virginia, Theresa, Phyllis (Dodo), Frank, and Joseph Soprano. Mama began treatments with Annamaria, who started her treatment by first making the sign of the cross over the child. She proceeded by praying to the Blessed Mother and the Sacred Heart of Jesus. Annamaria then made a poultice of beaten egg whites and a mixture of leaves and herbs. Some say Annamaria used prickly herbs from the sea to scrape Mama's eyes. She placed the egg poultice on the child's eyes, wrapping a clean white linen over them, like a blindfold. This procedure was done for several months or longer, four or five times a day. Doctors from Itri came to examine the child often, to ensure against infections.

Mama stayed at Annamaria's house at the start of her treatment. There were not any other answers for her; this treatment was the last resort. Only a miracle by the hands of this gifted woman could give Mama her eyesight. If God gave Annamaria this gift that was so profound, everyone believed God would give them a miracle.

There is a song I love that expresses the power of God: "God will make a way when there seems to be no way." Mama's grandparents believed in this powerful God. When Mama told me to write down the events, she was filled with bittersweet emotions of joy and sorrow. She talked about how she missed her mother. She said with tears rolling down her cheeks. "I would go into the barn and fall asleep in the hay holding Mama's picture, crying myself to sleep."

I can't imagine the terror this four-year-old blind child must have felt when being taken away from her mother through death. She found comfort and security in her father, sisters, and brothers (especially her brother, Alfonso, who cared for her in such a loving way). Going on a ship for a long journey to live with family in Italy who she never knew, and being left at the home of her grandparents, were traumatic events for her.

Her grandparents were well-known in the community for their own acts of charity to those who were sick and less fortunate, and the community prayed for and helped little Gaetanina.

Mama continued, "Everyone took Annamaria many eggs."

Many eggs were needed daily to make the egg white poultice for the treatment of Mama's eyes. If it meant bringing eggs to Annamaria, they did so with all of their hearts.

She said excitedly, "Grandpa [the person she loved most in the world] took me for a walk the day my bandages and blindfold came off, in the presence of family and friends in Itri Square. I started to cry. I had never seen anything before. Now, I was able to see."

Relatives and friends made every effort to help Gaetana and Alfonso in caring for Mama.

She continued to tell me, "A family friend, a town policeman, befriended me and walked with me daily. He would bring me confetti candies."

When Mama was finally able to go to the classroom, she recalled, "Enrico Cardi's cousin, Concillia, a schoolteacher, let me sit at her table to ensure I could see."

She loved her relatives and had close ties to them throughout her life. They were the family who knew, loved, and respected her.

Mama often talked about the kindness that her uncle Domenico's wife, Rosa, had shown to her. Rosa, Domenico, and their children lived in the Cardi home in Itri. She would tell me, "Zia Rosa (Mama called her Rosina) loved me. Hugging me, she would tell me she loved me." Often Rosa would hold the grieving child when she found her weeping, holding her mother's picture. She said emphatically, "Zia Rosina sewed clothes for me, Irene, and Aguila (Angie), her children. She would wash me and make sure I was clean." Mama loved Rosa and her family. They remained close to the day they passed. Rosa's daughters included Mama in many family events.

Mama talked about her Uncle Vincenzo. His wife, Lillian Rega, showed much kindness and friendship when Mama came to America. Zia Rosina and Zia Pasqualina (Lillian), and their families remained close to Mama and her children. We visited both homes often, and many of them - Catherine, Ida, and Lucy - frequently visited our home. It was as if we had older sisters. We remained close friends throughout our lives, along with their brothers Alphonse, John, James, and Ray. Mama treasured her relationships with her relatives, especially those who knew all the details of her life while living in Itri.

Rosa and Domenico Cardi
Photo: Ron Cardi

Peter, Fr. Roland, Angie, Irene, Paul, Alphonse, Rosa, Erminio, Elizabeth,
Mary, Nicholas, Domenico
Photo: Mary Barone

Lillian and Vincenzo Cardi

Ida, Katherine, John, Raymond Cardi

Lucy Cardi Di Fusco

Vincenzo Cardi's Connecticut Bar
Photo's: Roberta Di Marco

During one of my many visits to her home, Mary Barone told me the events of Domenico's tragic death. Reverend Roland Cardi was pastor of St. Ann's Church in North Providence. One day while driving towards his father's construction site not far from his parish, he noticed a crowd had gathered there. He stopped his car to inquire what was happening, only to find out that his father was buried under tons of sand. He administered the "last rites" of the Catholic Church to his own father.

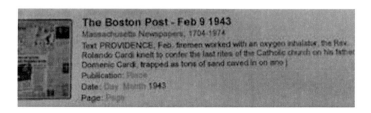

The Boston Post - Feb 9 1943
Massachusetts Newspapers, 1704-1974
Text PROVIDENCE, Feb. firemen worked with an oxygen inhalator, the Rev. Rolando Cardi knelt to confer the last rites of the Catholic church on his father Domenic Cardi, trapped as tons of sand caved in on one)
Publication: Place
Date: Day Month 1943
Page: Page

Immacolatina, Bisnonna Gaetana, Rosa, Baby (one of Rosa's)
Photo: Mary Barone

CHAPTER 5
LIFE WITH IMMACOLATINA

It seemed that life wasn't exactly easy for Mama in Itri. Alfonso and Gaetana's only daughter, Immacolatina, didn't like her niece, Gaetanina. She was jealous beyond words that the four-year-old blind girl had come to live with her parents. She couldn't tolerate Mama getting so much attention, because of her blindness. It was difficult for anyone to believe that Antonio's sister, who was married with her own children, would treat her niece so badly. Mama told me she was terrified of her.

Although Alfonso commanded Immacolatina to stop mistreating Gaetanina, she continued. Shortly after her four-year-old niece arrived in Itri, she grabbed the child and was about to throw her into the well on Alfonso's property, when family friends noticed the screaming child. They intervened and saved Mama once again. Immacolatina was relentless towards her niece. Her hatred and jealousy were palpable, and her plots were endless.

One day, Mama received a package from her father containing clothes and an umbrella. In a rage, Immacolatina stormed upstairs to Mama's bedroom and pulled her hair so hard, that blood came pouring down her face. Migelo's son (someone who lived in the Cardi home) ran upstairs to help the child. Then, Gaetana pulled her daughter away from her granddaughter. Bisnonno Alfonso ordered his daughter not to go anywhere near his granddaughter, ever again. Even so, in a rage, Immacolatina loudly vowed to all those present, that she would get Mama.

Sadly, when Gaetana passed away in 1927, her daughter couldn't resist further tormenting Mama, Roland, and the relatives who helped her. Seventeen years later, when Mama was twenty one and preparing to return to America, Immacolatina's next plot was to bring her niece and uncles to court.

Following are the court documents that Rosalba Martini Belfiore (Rome) translated from Italian into English:

In the Name of his Majesty

VITTORIO EMANUELE III
By the grace of God and the will of the nation, King of Italy, the magistrate of Fondi has handed down the following sentence.

These legal proceedings will not foresee public action.

AGAINST
1. Cardi Ascanio Ettore Teodoro di Antonio, 47 years old
2. Cardi, Caterina di Antonio, 21 years old
3. Cardi Antonio Salvatore fu Pasquale, 66 years old
All residents of Itri

All three ACCUSED of
Theft of a linen crate, of objects of gold and money appertaining to the inher-
itance of Maria Gaetana Pernarella, in damage to Immacolata Cardi, her
daughter, committed by three persons.

(Art. 401 and 404 Number 9 C.P.)
In Itri, October 15th, 1928-V11

THE FACTS

   With a statement, on the 10th of November, 1928, Immaculata Cardi of
Itri made a legal complaint against her niece Caterina Cardi (not living with
her) and two other relatives, Ascanio Cardi and Antonio Cardi, on the 15th
of October, 1928, accusing them of having stolen stealthily a certain amount
of linens, gold objects, and 10,000 lire, hiding the goods in a crate. All of these
items, which belonged to the deceased Maria Gaetana Pernarella, mother of
Immacolata Cardi.

   After a long and laborious preliminary investigation, the illustrious rep-
resentative of the king ruled out and excluded Antonio Cardi from the par-
ticipation in the delivery of the crate. Thus, article 404 of the Penal Code can't
be prosecutable and the case is postponed under the jurisdiction of the praetor
who will express his definite judgment.

THE RIGHTS OF LAW

Essentially, the few elements of which the accusation is based have been
supplied from the affirmations of the accuser and of the testimony, of very
little value, from Cleonice Agresti and Matilde Cardi. The first witness is
the tenant of the accuser and the other cousin of Immacolata Cardi. Matilde
Cardi declares that the transport of the linen crate to the Ascanio Cardi house
was commissioned by the three accused and physically carried out by the
carpenter, Giuseppe Meschino. She also declared that "very likely" the crate
could have contained the gold objects and the 10,000 lire that the deceased
Panarella had obtained as a result of the sale of a piece of land in Monte San
Biagio, four years prior. Taking turns, Cleonice Agresti and Matilde Cardi
assured that Mrs. Pernarella, a brief period of time before her death, possessed
a certain quantity of objects of gold, about which, however, they were not

able to describe the materials or characteristics. Indeed, the episode of the crate was able to be reconstructed in all of its details via the agreeing declarations of the testimonies of Doctor Angelo Saracini, Benedetta Sinapi, Guiseppe Meschino, and Vittorio Pecorone. They stated that following the death of her grandmother, Caterina Cardi, who had been close to her grandmother with whom she had lived, had to establish herself elsewhere. She asked her uncle Ascanio to bring to his house her few personal effects, which she had stored in a crate. After some hesitation, Cardi (Ascanio) opened the crate, showing the onlookers that what was contained inside was nothing but a few personal linens and an empty suitcase that belonged to his niece. Cardi explained that he had given the responsibility of arranging the transport to Giuseppe Meschino. Therefore, no secrecy surrounded the transport of the content and the transportation of the crate. In the presence of the witness Vittorio Pecorone, Ascanio Cardi implored the denouncer to recount that which she had kept in the famous crate. She responded, "What do I have to come to see, certainly there aren't marenghi (valuable gold coins)." The abundant testimony found in the investigation from both the prosecution and the defense demonstrated that the deceased Pernarella had found herself in a critical economic condition and was burdened with debts. Not only, but to quiet her most restless creditors, she had promised them their small payments as soon as she received a small amount of money from her sons who lived in America. Therefore, where would the 10,000 lire be that she had received from the sale of her land in Monte San Biagio? The approximate date of the sale is uncertain, but going by the testimony of the denouncer, and admitting that the sale had happened three or four years before the death of Pernarella, who can affirm that all of the obtained sums remained intact until the time of her death? According to an extract from the bank account book sent from Pernarella to Amedeo Cardi, there was a figure of an initial deposit of 4,500 lire dated the 13th of September 1924. Logically one has to admit that this money represents the residual of 10,000 lire in question, keeping in mind that the transfer of real estate sometimes happens as ordinarily happens for urgent economic necessity. It is easy to establish that, on October 15, 1928, the date of the death of Pernarella, from the 10,000 lire only 1,000 lire remained jealously guarded and deposited in a postal account. Also, for the objects of gold that they say were bound to Immacolata Cardi and about which Cleonice Agresti and Matilde Cardi spoke, it is impossible to establish their existence. From the testimony of many witnesses who were called on to testify (D'Alena, Vincenzo Maggiacomo, Vittoria Fargiuone, Antonio Soscio, Giovanna Spirito, etc.) the story emerges that Pernarella possessed only a long string of gold, two rings, and a pair of earrings of the same metal. If one considers that the above-stated objects were regularly inventoried and safeguarded, it is not clear what the other objects of gold would be. From all of the elements of the trial, one can affirm with certainty that neither linen, nor jewels, nor money were stolen. It was stated that Immacolata Cardi, prompted only by the gossip of a neighbor of the transport of the crate which happened in the middle of the night, was synonymous with a mischievous act. She was pushed in good faith to denounce and to take action against her niece and relatives, with whom she did not have a good relationship.

But wanting to believe in the existence of the objects of gold and of the 10,000 lire, it appears the method by which the theft would have taken place would be totally absurd! Who would want to seize the value of a small amount and easily hidden, would use a large crate, would verify it with four witnesses, would compromise the success of a good robbery, to take used linen? It would be childish and without sense. But Zia Immacolata believed she had been duped.

The innocence of the three defendants is obvious from every one of the pages of the trial. Ascanio Cardi and Antonio Cardi, honest and undefiled citizens of Itri, by the Vice Justice of the Peace, official of the Civil State: the other Director of Studies, presented that nothing was taken from the inheritance of Maria Gaetana Pernarella.

In the case of Caterina Cardi, one can exonerate her with a pronouncement of total innocence.

P.Q.M.
Doctor Mario Duni
Magistrate of Fondi
See articles 293 Capov. And 74 C p.p. It declares that there will be no trial proceeding against Ascanio Teodoro Cardi, Caterina Cardi, and Antonio Cardi for not having committed the crime attributed to them.
Fondi, June 19th,1929—VII

As part of the court proceedings, a complete professional inventory was taken of the estate of Gaetana Pernarella.

See Appendix for Continuation of the Inheritance Documents

The documents speak for themselves. As though it wasn't enough for Mama to endure these hardships, her pain and sadness were perpetuated when her family in America did not believe this story. It was only when some members of her family visited Italy years later that they learned of this terrible event, and finally acknowledged the extreme abuse their sister had endured at the hands of their aunt. They finally realized that their sister did not have the easy, glorious life they had thought she had.

Much of these memories have motivated me to bring this story and truth about her life to those whom she most loved. Whatever I have written cannot do justice to her life. I can only write the facts as told to me by Mama, Enrico Cardi, Zio Pasquale Cardi, and other Cardi relatives that lived in Itri. Knowing this story made me realize how deep and serious Mama's terror of her aunt was and of being arrested.

Mama explained emotionally, "When I boarded the ship to return to America, I was taken off the ship by two officers for using an assumed name, and for the theft of my grandmother's goods. My aunt reported and pressed charges against me."

She continued, "Because of my impeccable reputation and that of my grandparents, Zio Teodoro, and Zio Antonio, my uncles and I had much support in Itri. Our exemplary reputations were known in the courts."

I will always be grateful to Zio Teodoro and Zio Antonio Cardi for shielding Mama and withstanding much persecution from Immacolatina and her false witnesses.

The hurt and anger were very deep within Mama, Enrico, and his family. Enrico told me his family always remembered the sufferings and injustice his father, grandfather, and Mama had endured. For him, there was no forgiveness for someone who questioned their honor, and to put a stain on their names. This profound pain and suffering remained within him, as he told of these events and witnessing the intense difficulty his family and Mama endured.

He emotionally declared, "There is no forgiveness for what this evil woman did to my family, and your mother, for their honor to be questioned. We have not forgotten the hardship we went through because of her."

Zio Prof. Antonio Cardi, Recorder of Cardi ancestral history

Zio Ascanio (Teodoro) Cardi

Don Virgilio Mancini
Close childhood friend of Rev. Roland Cardi and Gaetanina

Bisnonno Alfonso, a successful merchant

CHAPTER 6
ALFONSO AND GAETANA'S
INFLUENCE

Even though Mama experienced much hardship, the influence of Alfonso and Gaetana was powerful in her upbringing.

Alfonso, a successful merchant and distinguished member of Itri, was honored and loved throughout Itri and beyond. He had a carriage business with fourteen horses and sold acqua minerale, chemicals, and many other goods throughout Italy.

Mama proudly explained, "When the cholera epidemic broke out in Terracina, Grandpa Alfonso donated many chemicals to kill the disease." She recalled that a plaque was erected in Alfonso's memory in the area of Terracina or Sperlongo. As a side note, Katherine, Ralph, and I tried to find it without success when we visited Terracina and Sperlongo many years ago.

Mama loved Sperlongo, Terracina, and Vendicia. She, her grandmother, and Roland spent their summers at the beach in Formia, called Vendicia (a short distance from Itri). Their donkey Cicciolo, took them with a 2-wheel buggy each day. When she spoke about her grandfather's driver, their horse, and beautiful carriage, her eyes would light up and be filled with love and longing. It was as if she had just returned home with her grandfather, from one of those charitable visits to the needy and ill, and she could smell the food cooking. She often described the large stove and oven she and Bisnonna Gaetana used for cooking.

Mama recalled, "My grandparents [Alfonso and Gaetana] entertained many priests from Itri and neighboring villages. Many monsignors and bishops ate grandma's food. If Roland had stayed in Italy, he would have been in the Vatican."

They lived a truly Christian life. Before eating dinner, Bisnonno Alfonso would take Mama with him to visit the sick and poor. He would load his carriage with medicine and the foods that Gaetana had prepared. When Bisnonno Alfonso and Mama returned home, they ate as a family, usually with many guests. When talking with our cousin, Alfonso Di Biase (son of Paolo Di Biase) during my trip to Itri in April 2013, he told me about the endless guests who went to the home of Gaetana and Alfonso for dinner, especially on Sundays.

As another side note, on New Year's Eve 2016, I received a message from our cousin Alfonso Di Biase that read, "I like to remember that our great-grandfather Alfonso, Christmas Eve, confraternity with many poor people who had no home, had dinner with them. Many people loved him."

That was Gaetana and Alfonso Cardi's legacy. They did all of this throughout their lives and shared their abundance with those less fortunate.

Mama continued this charitable practice throughout her life. She would give to others, even though she didn't have much for herself. She would tell her children, "Give, trust in God. He will provide." She lived her life with the solid belief of what Scripture tells us, "Give and gifts will be given to you; a good measure shaken down, and overflowing, will be poured into your lap. For the measure with which you measure, will, in turn, be measured out to you." (Luke 6: 39, New American Bible).

Lines of Pilgrims/Needy and Homeless at the Cardi Estate

Gaetanina (Mama) and Cosmo (Papa)

Capotosto Coat of Arm

CHAPTER 7
MEETING COSMO CAPOTOSTO/
PAPA (GAETANINA'S/MAMA'S
FUTURE HUSBAND/MY FATHER)

Onorato, born on October 30, 1865, was the son of Costanzo Capotosto and Regina Agresti, who lived in Itri. He married Benedetta Lorello, of Itri, on February 7, 1887. She was the daughter of Giuseppe Antonio Lorello and Maddelena Di Biase. Giuseppe's father was Andrea Lorello, and his mother was Benedetta Addessi. After the death of Benedetta, Onorato married Maria Concetta Meschino. Benedetta and Onorato had three children: Angelina (spouse Daniel Fusco), Vincenzo (first spouse Angela DelBove, second wife Amalia), and Cosmo (spouse Caterina/Gaetanina Cardi). Benedetta Lorello died when Papa was sixteen years old. Papa (Cosmo) lived with his father and his brother Vincenzo in Itri. Angelina was already married to Daniel Fusco and living in New York.

Papa was a Royal Guard at the Royal Castle in Caserta and a Military soldier at the Colosseum Amphitheater in Rome. Our brother, Aldo, was named after Papa's close friend, who was also a Royal Guard. He was a handsome, charming, and talented musician. He was a man of abundant talents and was gifted with many business skills. His business ideas were long before his time.

His family, who loved him, recognized his keen business abilities and creative skills. He loved his older sister, Angelina Capotosto Fusco, who lived in New York City with her family. When he visited America, he would live with her, as he prepared to become an American citizen. He would return to Itri after a stay with Angelina until he came to America permanently. Papa loved New York, and he seemed to thrive there. Aunts Rosario Cerrito, Maria Civita Sinapi, Giovanna Maria (Jennie) Fidelio, and uncles, along with his sister and her family, encouraged him to succeed in New York.

His uncle, Luca, came to America, on May 6, 1903. He arrived on the ship, Patria, and stayed with his sister Giovanna. Our grandfather, Onorato, and Luca came to America to work at the Barstow Stove Co. in New Jersey to earn money for their families. However, both men later returned to Itri to care for their families. The Capotosto family was close-knit and supportive of each other.

Papa petitioned for naturalization on July 1, 1926. His Aunt Maria Civita Capotosto Sinapi's husband, Luigi, and Louis Arzano sponsored him and were witnesses. He listed his work as a stove maker. The declaration stated that he was a resident of the United States since September 2, 1923. He was born in Itri on January 23, 1902, and the birth was registered in Caserta, Italy. He came to America on the vessel, Martha Washington, which sailed from Naples and arrived in Gloucester, New Jersey, September 2, 1923. His petition for citizenship was granted on May 13, 1928, at the age of 27. The records state that he lived at 141 East

13th Street, New York, the home of his sister, Angelina. He returned to Itri after receiving his citizenship.

Papa met Mama in Itri. One day, she and one of her friends walked to the piazza in Itri. It was July 21, in the mid-1920s at the feast of Maria Santissima della Civita. Papa, a resident of Itri who lived on Via San Gennaro, was at the feast of Maria Santissima della Civita. Papa, was standing in the piazza with Don Francesco Sinapi (Zio Lugino Sinapi's brother).

Don Francesco said to Mama, "Good evening, miss. Your father was my friend."

Mama described how Papa was dressed to a tee. She said, "He wore white, wide-bottom pants, with a tight top, and a navy-blue jacket. His shoes were white and blue. I looked at him and called him, il pagliaccio [clown].

As she and her friends continued to walk, she asked, "Who is that pagliaccio?"

Papa was known for the sharp way in which he dressed and was called a sheik. He usually dressed in a dress shirt and tie, mainly bow ties, and on occasion, he dressed casually.

Each day, Papa and Don Francesco would sit in front of her house to get her attention. Papa had yet another nickname, Bill. He would serenade Mama each day with his guitar or mandolin, as she peered out the window or watched from the balcony. Her first impression of him began to change, and gradually the couple began courting with supervision, with intentions to marry.

Mama had plans to return to America before her planned marriage. Records show that she was booked to board the vessel, Conte Biancamano, with an arrival date in America of November 1928, a year before her marriage to Papa. However, her journey was canceled due to the charges made against her, as explained in a previous chapter.

Cosmo (Papa)

Cosmo (Papa) Military Soldier, Colosseum, Rome and Royal Guard at Royal Castle, Caserta, Italy

Zio Vincenzo, Nonna Benedetta, Zia Angelina, Nonno Onorato, Cosmo

Acting honorably, according to Italian tradition, Papa went to America to seek the blessing of Antonio and Maria Battista for his planned marriage to Mama. He arrived at the Cardi home in Cranston to meet Antonio. Maria Battista and Antonio were furious. They didn't approve of this match. They had plans for her to marry Maria Battista's nephew, Angelo, or a friend of her brother, Alfonso.

Mama explained, "I could not marry Angelo. We were close friends; our relationship and love for each other were that of a brother and sister."

They were in a predicament. It wasn't proper for an unmarried couple to travel alone, without a chaperone, especially on a long voyage. They had no other choice than to marry in Italy. Papa went back to Itri to marry Mama, without parental approval. The couple were married in Itri, at the Church of the Annunziata, now named Santa Maria Maggiore on Wednesday, September 16, 1929, on the anniversary of her grandfather's death. Don Salvatore Mancini officiated the wedding. Zio Teodoro and Zia Loreta, Enrico's parents, attended. Teodoro said, "State and church come together."

Passport

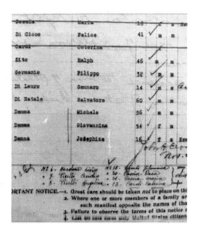

Cancellation passenger list for Conte Biancamano
Caterina Cardi is listed. (Ellis Island)

Santa Maria Maggiore Church

Others who were present were Don Francesco Sinapi and several of Papa's relatives. She didn't mention any others. It seemed very few approved of this match, which took a toll on Mama. Even so, they were married and decided to go to the states, especially since Papa was already a citizen and had relatives in New York City.

When their ship arrived at Ellis Island, there were thousands of people waiting to greet their relatives and friends. Mama searched for her father, thinking he would be there to greet the daughter he hadn't seen in 20 years. It was customary for families to greet their loved ones on a voyage like this.

Even knowing of her family's disapproval, Papa believed they would be there. Papa said to her, "I'm not going to tell you who your father is; you pick him out."

They waited and waited, searched and searched, and never found him. Not Antonio, or any other member of his family went to greet Mama. She wept unceasingly. It was another rejection for her. Neither of them imagined this outcome. Nonetheless, they proceeded with their plans.

Papa's family, on the other hand, went to the ship to welcome the newly married couple, as well as Maria Civita Sinapi's daughter Lottie, and son, Tom.

There was a party at Zia Giovanina's house and Mama expressing joy said, "They threw confetti at me." The couple was greeted with open arms by all of Papa's relatives. They urged the couple to stay in New York, where they knew Papa would have many opportunities with his talents and business skills.

Papa wanted them to live in New York with his sister, Angelina, and other relatives and friends, where he had already established himself, but Mama wanted to be with the family she had only known as a child. She longed to know her father, sisters, and brothers.

Mama explained, "Papa [Cosmo/my father] and I left for Knightsville after a brief stay in New York." She sadly said, "Again, I thought my family would come to greet me when the ship arrived in Providence, but only my sister, Civitina, and my father [Antonio] came. When we arrived at Papa's [Antonio's] house, my sister Annie was there. Alfred and Americo were working. Uncle Arthur Crudale who was working in the A. Cardi Construction Co. garage greeted me with a handshake. Papa [Cosmo] did not get any greeting."

Mama said, "My sister Anna wanted to give me a party, but Antonio said, 'No, it's over.'"

Several months later, Grandpa Antonio must have been persuaded by family members to change his mind about a party for Mama and Papa, because Mary Cardi Barone (Mama's cousin) remembers going to a party for them, where relatives gathered to greet the couple.

The couple needed to establish themselves in a new country. Antonio had housed several of his relatives and friends when they first came to America. His daughter who he had not seen in many years, was back home. She and her husband needed housing. Papa, who was new to Knightsville, did not have the connections he would have had in New York, to find housing or work. Finally, Grandpa Antonio allowed Mama and Papa to rent the first floor of his multi-unit tenement house. He and Grandma Maria Battista lived upstairs with their daughter, Maria Civitina. Aunt Anna Migliori lived on the third floor with her husband Joseph, and children, Julius and Anna. His property was referred to as Cardi's yard.

Capotosto aunts and uncles from New York and New Jersey
Cerrito, Fidelio, Sinapi:
Photo: Maryann Sinapi Peterson

Antonio gave Papa a laborers job in his construction company. Working as a laborer was difficult for Papa due to frequent episodes of Malaria. Being a laborer was not his forte. After a time, he began working at the Cranston Print Works.

Papa worked hard and struggled alone, to create a more suitable profession for himself over time, while still working at The Cranston Print Works. He was a man of abundant talents, and he loved to create. He became known for his unique formulas of household items, such as bleach water, floor wax, and disinfectants which he developed over the years. He was especially known for his bleach water, which he sold for ten cents a gallon. He was a master at the import and export business and was creative with ceramic figurines, which he made from molds. He was also the local taxidermist. His passion was music, and he was a master at playing the guitar and mandolin. Our family has fond memories of him serenading Mama while playing the Italian Neapolitan song *Cateri*, on his mandolin. Musicians came from across Rhode Island to have him tune their instruments before they played at a public place. Besides playing his instruments, many in Knightsville loved to hear him whistle. Friends and neighbors gave him another nickname, The Whistler. His talents were endless.

The pear tree where tenants, relatives, and friends gathered was at the heart of Cardi's yard, the center, the community gathering place where we all met, played, socialized, sang, danced, planted gardens, and entertained visitors, especially relatives from New York. People remember many things about their childhood. The children of Itrani immigrants who lived in Cardi's yard remember fondly our times under the pear tree.

His cousin, Ida Corpolongo Soprano, whose grandmother Allessandrana was a Lorello, (Nonna Benedetta's father's sister), recently talked about Papa and her memories of him. She described him as a dignified, classy, talented man. Ida was sponsored to come to America by Santina Soprano and lived in an apartment over Knightsville Loan, at the corner of Park Avenue and Cranston Street, a bank owned by Frank Sinapi, close to our home.

One Sunday, hearing a knock, she opened her door to see Papa standing there with a loaf of freshly baked Italian bread. He introduced himself and said, "I am good friends with your father, and we are cousins on your mother's side of the family."

Ida asked her father about Papa, and he responded by telling his daughter, "Yes, indeed we are close friends and relatives. He is a talented musician, especially with the mandolin and guitar."

Ida continued expressing great admiration for Papa. "He would come to my apartment to bring me a loaf of freshly baked bread each Sunday morning. If I wasn't home, he would leave it at my door."

Mama and Papa quickly adjusted in the new environment. They became acquainted and re-acquainted with many relatives and families from Itri. Their home was always opened to everyone, especially relatives who needed their help often and were illiterate. They were able to celebrate with family and community, the feast the Itrani community held scared. The feast to their Madonna della Civita was celebrated in Itri and in Knightsville every year on July 21st. It was a sacred day for the Itrani immigrants in Cranston.

Jubilee of the Coronation of Maria Santissima della Civita

Itrani immigrants marching from St. Rocco's Church early 19ᵗʰ century with the original statue of the Madonna della Civita

CHAPTER 8
FEAST OF THE MADONNA
DELLA CIVITA

Yearly, Mama and Papa welcomed Papa's family from New York City. Papa's aunt Maria Civita and uncle Luigino Sinapi would come for the feast, and for many years spent the summers with our family, until they were no longer able to travel. Their son, Frank, and his wife, Ann, visited each year until they were physically unable. This holiday was celebrated by my parents, ancestors, and all of the people from Itri whether they lived in Knightsville, Itri, or other states and countries.

The sanctuary in Itri and the painting of the Civita, share a millenary history. The Itrani community continues to feel blessed and proud that heaven chose Mount Civita in Itri, to manifest a miracle.

The folk tradition narrates that a deaf and dumb shepherd found the sacred image as he was in search of one of his lost cows in the bushes of Mount Civita in the year 796. The image was among the branches of a holm oak tree where the cow was kneeling, and at that moment, the shepherd regained his voice and hearing. This is how the history and the Civitana devotion begin. The origins of this painting and how it got there is a mystery, being the place was so inaccessible. Many authors believed that St. Luke the Evangelist was the author of the painting due to the presence of three letters LMP placed at the base of the picture. LMP stands for "Lucas Me Pinxit." (Pecchia 2003).

In 1527, Itri was decimated by an epidemic of pestilence, and the painting of the Civita was taken in procession through the streets of Itri. The people implored *their* Madonna that the infectious disease would come to an end. Suddenly during the procession, they saw a cloud lift from the ground, and it dissipated in the air. The disease came to an end. In memory of this event, the date established to celebrate annually the *Civita*, and her first crowning was July 21. (Pecchia 2003).

I am proud to have witnessed the profound faith, commitment, and love of the elders for *their* Madonna. They have continually left us with the message to pass on their faith and traditions. Many of us have. I'm in awe when I think about the image appearing in a tree in Itri. It seemed that heaven chose Itri for the home of this sacred image. How blessed we are to have this heritage.

Roughly 60 years ago, when most of us were young and still single, we, along with all of our relatives, celebrated St. Mary's festivities at Uncles Rico and Alfred Cardi's home on Oaklawn Avenue. Our aunts, Jeanette and Alene, invited many friends and family to celebrate with them. An abundance of food and drink were savored by all of us, as we heard the music in the background.

Painting by St Luke of the Civita

The Miracle

In keeping with their tradition to celebrate the feast, as their parents did, Stephen and Tony Cardi invite family members and friends to Antonio's Restaurant each year to join with them in the celebration with a gourmet dinner, music, and the retelling of historical facts about our feast.

Our family and most Itrani families have a deep devotion and faith to the Madonna della Civita, which is celebrated each year on, or the Sunday closest to, July 21st. It is one of our favorite feast days. This, sacred tradition was brought to us by the Itrani immigrants. Their feast was revered by them, and no sacrifice was too big for them to celebrate the feast of *their* Madonna. Members of our community attend what originally was a week-long novena, as the immigrants did in the early 1900s 'til it was changed to a three-night service in and about 2015.

During the week before the feast, Phenix Avenue is blocked off, and vendors sell a variety of foods and articles. Various bands perform in the square under the gazebo (where the Cranston City Hall once stood), as they did years ago in the open space.

To celebrate the feast, many Itrani people who live in other states come in buses, while others fly or drive to Rhode Island. Often, they stay with relatives who live in Rhode Island or simply come for the Mass and procession. In the years before St. Mary's Church was built, in the early 1900s, the feast began at the Italian church of St. Rocco's in Thornton. The immigrants would process with the first, original statue of their Madonna, from St. Rocco's to Knightsville. After the procession, their statue of the Madonna would be brought back to St Rocco's to be stored in a nave above the altar, until the following year. For reasons unknown, the original statue was never taken to the newly built St. Mary's.

While researching the history of St. Mary's Church in 1975, I found the statue. Ralph and I restored it three times over the years from 1975-1999. In the years following, I would touch up the statue when needed. Father Farina, the pastor of St. Mary's Church, did not want the statue when I found it. It remained in my home for thirty-six years. Finally, in 2011, with the help of Larry Baldino, the statue was accepted at St. Mary's Church by the pastor Reverend James Verdelotti and was placed on the left side altar.

The original statue of the Civita, St. Rocco's Church
Photo: Reverend Angelo Carusi

Bernadette restoring the statue. Nephew Matthew Izzo watching
Original statue of the Civita

Original statue of the Civita (1905). Left Side altar at St.Mary's Church

Years before, in the early 1900s, the ten o'clock High Mass was celebrated at St. Rocco's Church, until in the mid to late 1900s the Italian
immigrants were able to go to St. Ann's Church in Cranston. The ten
o'clock High Mass was preached by our dear pastor Father Cesare Schettini, a well-known orator. When St. Mary's Church was established in
1935, the Mass and novena was held there. After Mass, the statue of the
second Madonna was and still is brought out into the street, as hundreds of people gather to participate in the long procession. Thousands
stand on the sidewalks, waiting patiently for the procession and the
Madonna to approach them. In years past, men would bid one hundred
dollars for the honor of carrying the statue. A band precedes the statue,
and one will see many of the church societies with their banners. There
are floats, politicians, at times the Shriners, and other local bands and
groups. Many reverent parishioners, visitors, and priests can be heard
praying the rosary. The Itrani women sing loudly the Italian hymns from
their native land, especially Evviva Maria, as they march throughout the
streets of Knightsville.

During the procession, people offer water or lemonade to those who
are marching. Most participants refuse anything to drink as the elders
did in the beginning days of our celebration in the 19th century. Some
march without drinking for the duration of the procession. I distinctly
remember some elders marched with bare feet, long black dresses, and
some marched on their knees. How they did this is difficult to believe,
because the streets were extremely hot from the July sun. This encounter
was not easy to forget. The deep faith and reverence of our elders were
unforgettable.

As children, in the 1940s, and beyond, the girls in our family, close
relatives, and friends dressed in their First Communion dresses and
marched with the elders. We didn't have any choice; it was mandatory.
The young boys marched in their St. Anthony robes made by Madeline
Pallotta.

Madeline had three children: Arthur, Antonio, and Theresa. The
Pallotta family lived next door to our family, in one of Antonio's apartments. She was an expert seamstress and made the most beautiful dresses

for Theresa. Theresa too was like an older sister to me. While visiting their home, Madeline would offer me her delicious apple crisp which was an added treat. It was the best I had ever eaten.

Arthur, Madeline's elder son, marched as an altar boy. He worked at Medical Arts Pharmacy from an early age. Uncle Alfred taught him everything about pharmaceuticals and managing the pharmacy. Tony Pallotta a toolmaker told me one morning while we were having coffee, that his uncle James Pastore visited their home often. James was an expert tailor and a friend of Father Schettini. The two would argue about the Catholic faith. Mr. Pastore read and followed the Bible but was not sold on Catholicism. Tony has a great memory and is a good storyteller.

Neighborhood boys in St. Anthony robes

Mary Palumbo marching with Theresa Soprano,
Anna Migliori, and Bernadette

Madeline Pallotta
Photo: Tony Pallotta

Arthur Pallotta

Tony Pallotta and Bernadette talking about days past

Participants in the procession pray for a miracle for a loved one, for a parishioner who is facing a life and death situation, or simply to honor their Madonna. From 1970 until the 1990s, I would place a 100-foot rosary made of boating rope, and artificial red and blue roses, in the procession. I made the rosary for the diocesan rosary rally that I chaired in the 1970s. Our guest speaker was the Venerable Reverend Patrick Peyton. Our family's children, parishioners, local men, and women marched with the rosary, praying for an answer to their prayers.

Capotosto, Cardi, Conte, Izzo, LaTour, Vartanian and children from various parishes carrying the 100 ft. rosary

Family Children, and parishioners carrying the 100 ft. rosary

The Contes with the Venerable Father Patrick Peyton

Mama marching in the procession with Caroline Curelli,
Phyllis Ricci (Dodo), and Hilda Scaralia

Mama marched in the procession in her years while living in Itri and throughout her life in America. When she went anywhere, she carried a heavy handbag. I would plead with her not to carry her handbag, especially as she marched each year during our feast. She would angrily tell me or one of my sisters, "Mind your business, I need it." Of course, one of us would end up carrying it for her. Carrying her handbag during the feast was not easy. The march was long, it was and is usually a scorching hot day, and ends 2 or more hours later.

Sometimes, I would open her bag to see what made it so heavy and decide what I could remove. You might think that she had millions of dollars in it, but her millions were her precious prayer books, with many prayer cards of different saints, or the memorial cards of deceased friends and family members, inserted into the pages. There were rosary beads in the event she wanted to give any away, pictures of her grandchildren, and great-grandchildren, Life Saver candy, lemon and fruit drops, gum, and change with a few dollars to give to her grandchildren, great-grand-children, or anyone else's children. Her small amount of money seemed to multiply as she generously gave it away, never worrying where she would get additional money for her needs. I have never known another human being who could love and relate to children the way Mama did.

Mama, like all of the Itrani community, honored the yearly feast of the Madonna. She would place a table, clothed with a white linen embroidered cloth, in front of the former Medical Arts Pharmacy Building. Baskets of fresh flowers, brought by me, my sisters and Cardi relatives, were and still are placed on the table, as we wait for the Madonna. Many of our Cardi relatives, and former neighbors gather in front of the Cardi Building waiting for the Madonna to approach. The men carrying the statue stop, and the table is taken out into the street (this tradition dates back to the beginning with our Cardi grandparents, early 1905). The men who carry the Madonna place the statue on the table. People gather around the statue of the *Civita*, and flowers are strewn upon her. It's touching to see the emotions of her people as they beg for a miracle, or to simply thank her.

Mama marched in the procession until she had a stroke in her early 90s. After her stroke, Cosmo would take her to the feast. She sat in a wheelchair watching the procession and greeting many friends and relatives, as Aunt Jeanette and Uncle Rico Cardi also did in their last years.

The procession ends with the Madonna entering the church again. The men who carry the statue place her on the side altar in front of the church. The spiritual portion of the feast concludes with the benediction.

Zoë Conte and Kristiana Giannini

Men placing the Madonna on a table

Marie placing flowers on the Civita

Cosmo and Mama waiting in front of the Cardi Building for the Civita

*Aunt Jeanette and Uncle Rico waiting in front of the
Cardi building for the Civita*

The fun portion of the feast starts during the week of the novena. Phenix Avenue is blocked off, and vendors sell a variety of foods and articles. Various bands perform in the square under the gazebo (where the Cranston City Hall once stood), as they did in the beginning years in the open space. Many of the local children wait impatiently to get their cotton candy or doughboy, as was the case when our children and grandchildren were young. On the property behind the Civita Center, carnival rides are erected. One can find hundreds of families, and children begging and tormenting their parents or grandparents to allow them to go on all of the rides. Their cries and pleas are endless.

Of course, Ralph and I would always give in to our children and grandchildren when they were young in the 1960s-1990s. We spent a small fortune on tickets for the carnival rides, and the dart games, so that each child could win a stuffed animal or token to take home. We rationalized that this only happened once a year, during our special feast celebration.

The festivities end on Sunday evening. Hundreds of people gather throughout the streets, fields, and backyards to watch the culmination of a colorful display of fireworks.

The entire community was and still is involved in our feast. This day continues to be a holy day for the Itrani community. When I think back at how it was when we were growing up in comparison to how it is today, I marvel at the past effort, participation, and deep faith and commitment the Itrani community had for their feast day, to honor their Madonna. Having so little for themselves and their families, they gave all that they had on that day.

Festivities continue as families, their many friends, and out of state visitors celebrate in the backyard of a relative or friend. The food and drink are endless, and a sight to behold. As one walks by a person's yard, music can be heard, and one could hear the joy of people laughing and having fun. As in past days, homes are open to everyone. It was a time of great joy for all of us then and still is today. After our marriage, and when we had our own home, for years Ralph and I hosted the feast at our home or the homes of my sisters. It's a tradition we prayed would be carried on by our children and grandchildren for all generations. It is sad for those of us who are the elders now, to witness much indifference towards our feast and the church.

The years of research that I have done, for my published book *Eviva Maria, Madonna della Civita* left me with a longing to memorialize the Itrani immigrants, and our ancestors for their sacrifices, work, and faith to preserve our history. They were determined to give their families every opportunity to succeed, and to have a church where they could worship freely. To me, our ancestral history is extraordinary and needs to remain alive.

Over the years, I had dreamed of establishing a memorial in honor of the Itrani immigrants, or a small museum where all of my biographical notes and those of others, could be displayed for future generations. It did not become a reality in Cranston, Rhode Island. Recently, I met with the former mayor of Itri, Giovanni Ialongo, and the Mayor of Itri, Antonio Fargiorgio when they visited Cranston. I expressed to Mayor Fargiorgio that I would gladly give him the biographical notes taken from my book *Eviva Maria, Madonna della Civita*, if he established a memorial or museum in honor of the Itrani immigrants. He agreed and expressed his desire to do something for all of the Itrani immigrants. He asked for my approval to have my book translated and published in Italian.

Bernadette presenting her book, Eviva Maria, Madonna della Civita to Mayor Antonio Fargiorgio. Photo: Ron Cece

Presenting my biographical notes to Mayor Fargiorgio. Simone Fargiorgio
(C) (Providence Journal, November 27, 2018)

AVV. Antonio Fargiorgio
Mayor of Itri
March 19, 2019

Dear Mayor, Fargiorgio:
I, Bernadette M. Conte, residing in Cranston, Rhode Island, USA, authorize Mayor Antonio Fargiorgio, the publication of my biographical notes taken from: "Eviva Maria, Madonna della Civita," for the sole purpose of establishing a museum or memorial in honor of the Itrani immigrants, with the following references: Bernadette M. Conte, author, daughter of Caterina (Gaetanina) Cardi her husband Cosmo Capotosto, granddaughter to Maria Civita Saccoccio and Antonio B. Cardi.

Sincerely,

Bernadette M. Conte

Papa, Mama, Maria Civita and Luigino Sinapi with Capotosto children–under the pear tree

CHAPTER 9
OUR FAMILY

After three years of marriage, the couple began to have a family. Within the years of 1930-1937, five of her children, Luke, Aldo, Benedetta, and the twins, Anna and Marie, were born in the same house at 1707 Cranston Street, Cranston, Rhode Island.

Anna and Marie were twins. Mama periodically would tell us a story about Luke. She was pregnant with twins and told Luke to put pennies in her shoe. She told him, "If you place the pennies in my shoe, a baby will come to us." He placed two pennies in her shoe. Luke said he had placed the pennies under his pillow, but Marie and I remember that Mama told us they were placed in her shoe. She said, "On Mother's Day,

May 9, I gave birth to twins." She would tell Luke, "You put two pennies in my shoe, now you have two babies."

Luke, the first-born son and, oldest child, loves music and carves birds out of soap bars, wood, or simply makes anything. He is gifted with diesel engines and has won many awards for his winemaking. He is well known and respected within the trucking community which he serviced. His company (before his retirement) repaired diesel engines. I call him the man with the "golden hands." He has many hobbies, including traveling. He, like Marie, is knowledgeable about alternative medicine. Luke is well versed in many topics, and never sits still. He is constantly on the go. After a brief conversation, he will simply say, "Okay, I have to go, I have so much to do."

He married Rita Cuomo of Caserta, Italy, the daughter of Imperia Palazzo and Guglielmo Cuomo. It was love at first sight for them. Rita immediately became part of our family and our children had a special relationship with her. Mama and Papa loved her and treated her as if she were their daughter. Rita had two brothers, Mario and Frank, and a sister Dora. Luke and Rita had three children: Rita, Luke, and Dora. Rita has graduate degrees in Mental Health Counselling and School Psychology. She is Vice President of Family Development in Rhode Island. Dora is a social worker, and Luke worked in his father's business.

After the death of Rita in 1999, Luke would visit Ralph and me each night for dinner. One-night Ralph said, "Luke, I know you don't drink, but why don't you learn how to make wine. Make it, and I'll be the taster." That was the beginning of a new and successful career for Luke. He has won hundreds of first place ribbons and awards for his wine.

Luke began to research and learn about winemaking. He joined wine clubs, began to know many people who make wine, and learned about the various types of grapes to use for different wines. He has become well respected, and younger men seek out his knowledge and advise in their venture to make wine. He cherishes his time with his companion Barbara Mederios, who also makes wine with him.

Luke and Rita

Antonetta and Luke Cosmo Capotosto family

Rita Capotosto, Sam and daughter, Jacqueline Brunner

Jeff and Dora Gaudreau

Jeff Gaudreau

Aldo was the second son and child. His profession was in electronics, and as a hobby, he would at times use the skills Papa taught him in taxidermy. Aldo went out with Papa often to deliver goods to stores, and bleach water to many homes. He was a champion wrestler at Cranston High School [now Cranston East]. He loved fancy, gourmet, non-Italian foods, which I loved to make for him. I tried every recipe I learned in home economics classes on Aldo. He was the gentlest, kindest person one could have known. He was loved by all of us and would do anything for anyone.

Aldo had a simple method of pulling a loose tooth. One end of a long string would be tied around the loose tooth, and the other end tied around a doorknob of an open door. When Aldo would slam the door shut, the tooth would come out. He pulled cousin Anna Migliori Ferri's tooth one night when she came downstairs to our apartment. We all stood around her, waiting for her reaction. She was in shock, as she gazed in amazement at the tooth in her hand. It happened so fast; she did not feel any pain.

Our family was both proud and elated that Luke and Aldo met in Germany during the Korean War. Aldo was gravely injured in Germany. He never told Mama, Papa, or any of us. He went through all the trauma and surgeries alone. His jugular vein was cut, and he went through the threat of death without family.

I will never forget when our family went to meet him at the train station. Our excitement quickly turned into shock. His facial scars were many and deep. He needed many plastic surgeries that he had in a military hospital in New Jersey. Luke would drive our family to visit Aldo each week. It was a hard time for our family, and for him.

Aldo at the A. Cardi garage

Aldo

Aldo and Luke meet in Germany

Aldo was the first sibling to pass on January 25, 2001, of non-Hodgkin's Lymphoma. It was heartbreaking to see our mother in the sorrow and grief that only a mother feels at the loss of her child. Aldo and Mama lived with Cosmo in his home. Cosmo and Mama had a painful time adjusting to the loss of Aldo. It was a difficult time for all of us, especially Cosmo when Mama became ill again and had to be hospitalized. She never recovered from the loss of her son. She passed eleven months later.

I recall one of my conversations with Anna Migliori Ferri regarding Uncle Alfonso's death. Aunt Annie told her, "Grandpa Antonio never got over the loss of his first son, Dr. Alfonso." She continued, "The grief and heartbreak were so deep, that he collapsed and died of a massive heart attack three years later, while sweeping the sidewalk in front of the Medical Arts Pharmacy.

Mama reminded me frequently, that when she was pregnant with her third child, Papa hoped for a girl. He would give her his mother's name, *Benedetta*. His love for his mother was deep, and he strongly felt the loss of her.

I was that girl. Unfortunately, a district nurse began calling me Bertha. She thought Benedetta was too long and difficult to remember. The alias name that I immensely dislike stuck with me throughout my life. Papa would continually tell me to use my legal name. Most of the kids I knew in school would laugh and make fun of me when I referred to myself as Benedetta. Being shy, I gave up trying until I became an adult. The name Bertha has remained to the present day.

After giving birth to Cosmo, Mama returned home from the hospital and was confined to bed for a long time. I was ten-years old, the oldest girl and middle child, when Cosmo was born. Papa kept me home from school for a month, to take care of Mama and the baby. This is when I started my cooking career for our family. Papa taught me how to make gravy and meatballs. I discovered that I liked cooking. Mama would remark, "You have to learn everything." So, I did learn the Gaetanina and Gaetana way.

I owe my adventurous spirit to Papa. When I was fifteen years old, he told me I would be going to New York City to attend his niece Lorraine Fusco's wedding. He made arrangements for me to stay with his sister, Angelina, and cousin, Bessie, for a month. Papa took me to the train station and told me when I arrived at Penn Station, his niece Bernadette (Bessie) would be there. Before the train came, he held me by the shoulders, looked into my eyes, and said firmly but gently, "Benedetta, from this day on, you will represent me in my family, promise me." I replied, "Yes Papa, I promise." I kept the promise I made to Papa. I attended every wedding, funeral, family gatherings, and events for all of his relatives, traveling by train in the rain, sleet, snow, blizzards, and heat.

I stayed with our cousin, Albert Fusco, and his wife Yolanda, an artist, many times when I attended a family funeral. They were loving and interesting. I was the recipient of much wisdom from Yolanda. I saw Mae, Lorraine (ill with severe heart disease), and her son David, cousins Dannie (Junior), and Bobbie when I visited Bessie and Aunt Angelina, who lived next door to Lorraine.

My month-long visit to New York was fun. I experienced a lifestyle that was new to me, and I loved it. Bessie (we were all extremely close to her) took me to her special places to buy clothes, and to go out to eat. When Bessie ordered a drink, it was the first time I had ever heard of martini's or Manhattan's. Holding her glass up Bessie said, "Take a sip." I did and told her I thought it was awful. She laughed, as she continued to enjoy her drink. Maryann and Patty Sinapi took me to Coney Island, where I was coaxed to go on a roller coaster for the first time. Not knowing what to expect, I felt as if I would die of fright. Mischievous Patty laughed, knowing she pulled a fast one on me.

Our cousin, Mae Fusco, taught me how to fry peppers by adding Hunt's tomato sauce. I had never heard of Hunt's sauce until then. Visiting New York was a wonderful, memorable experience for me, even though Aunt Angie was strict. She didn't allow me to do anything she thought Papa would disapprove of. Luke and Aldo spent some summers in New York with the Sinapis and Fuscos, which they also treasured, especially when Frank took them to Coney Island. In later years, Mama, Anna, Marie, and I would take the train to New York, and occasionally visit Bessie and Aunt Angelina. When Zia Maria Civita and Zio Lugino Sinapi were living, we would climb the stairs to their third-floor apartment to visit with them, and with their son Frank and his wife Ann, who lived next door. Our family had close ties to Anna and Frank. We looked forward to seeing them each year, for our feast of the Madonna della Civita.

On several occasions while in New York, the Sinapis took me to see Frank's brother Eddie, who was a cameraman for the filming of many big-time movies made on the streets of New York City. It was exciting for a teenager to see a movie being made and having a relative be a part of the production.

I can see why many of the younger generations in our family are gifted in writing books, screenplays, producing plays, movies, and being involved in the arts. The genes are certainly from all sides of our family DNA.

Hardly anyone is left now. Over the years, several times a year until recently, I went to New York to meet with our cousin, Maryann Sinapi Peterson.

Maryann Sinapi Peterson

Maryann and her husband Artie, who live in Bronxville, a beautiful residential section of the Bronx, would insist I stay with them for an overnight, or several days. Until her recent retirement, Maryann worked at a large travel agency and was a travel consultant to many important corporate clients and company executives. I would take the bus or train with her into the city. Several years ago, around 2015, at the insistence of Maryann, I stayed with the couple when I went to Mt. Sinai Hospital to meet with a world-renowned heart surgeon. I was grateful to both of them for their hospitality. Maryann was gracious enough to accompany me for my consultation at Mt. Sinai Hospital, before the scheduled date of my open-heart surgery.

Papa had his plans and hopes for my career. I wanted to be a cosmetologist. He did not like the idea of me touching people's heads and did not want me to become a cosmetologist. Papa wanted me to follow in his footsteps and become a businesswoman. I didn't understand what he wanted for me, because I didn't want to spend long hours in his store. I didn't have the opportunity to participate in after-school clubs and programs. The long hours were lonely for me.

My only solace was reading the books I obtained from the local Knightsville library. I spent time listening to the radio, as I sang with a song sheet in hand, to the music of Nat King Cole, Patti Page, Dean Martin, Frank Sinatra, Fats Domino, Joni James, Sara Vaughn, and other well-known artists of our day. I took great care of the small radio; it was my salvation. To occupy my boredom, I would look out the window and count the cars and people that went by. I was petrified of an old man who was the father of one of our tenants, who on several occasions tried to get into the store, pushing on the locked door. When Papa came to get me in the evening, I would tell him how frightened I was of this man. He warned Mr. Silva never to go near me again.

Papa would take me to the gift shows when I was eleven or twelve years old, and proudly asked me to take his arm. I was young and didn't quite like going to gift shows with Papa. I would rather have been out playing with the neighborhood kids or my friends. I detested the loneliness of sitting in his store for hours on end after school, into the night, and all-day Saturdays. I wanted to be outside with my friends and siblings, or attend after-school events, which I never could do. The Knightsville Library and books became my best friends. I didn't understand what he was trying to teach me until I was older. He simply wanted me to learn everything about imports and exports and become a businesswoman. Most anyone would have been grateful for acquiring this knowledge, but I was too young, and just wanted to be the child I was.

In my later years, I realized what Papa was trying to teach me. His guidance became useful to me over the years. To this day, I have an interest in the import, export business, and regret not listening to him.

After high school graduation, I had little choice but to work as an account receivable bookkeeper and dispatcher for A. Cardi Construction Co. I wanted to work in the city, go to college, and continue on a different path. My parents agreed with Uncle Alfred's decision that I should work for him. They liked the thought that I would work close to our home. The matter had been discussed and decided. I didn't have any say in the decision. Luke worked as a mechanic for A. Cardi Construction Co. Our wages were little to nothing. My pay was fifty cents an hour. I later worked three jobs just so I could go to cosmetology school.

One day as I was sitting at my desk, Uncle Alfred Cardi, called me into his office. He firmly insisted that I correct any documents I had with the name Bertha. He advised, "Young lady, I baptized you as Benedetta. Bertha is not your name. Correct it, so one day your children will not have a problem if you acquire property." Without anyone knowing it, I went to the city hall and changed my name to Bernadette. My name was more modern now, and I was hoping people would find it easier to call me by my legal name. Mama was furious with me. She said, "If your father was alive, he would be in a rage with you. Your name is Benedetta. He named you after his mother, you made a big mistake." She was right, I was impulsive and anxious to delete "Bertha" out of my life. A name I still dislike each time I hear it and when listing it as an alias.

Anna Gloria Capotosto Izzo

Ralph, Bernadette, Ronald, and Anna Izzo

Anna was Marie's twin. A neighborhood boy was relentless in harassing and bullying my sisters and me one day when we were outdoors playing. To our surprise, Anna punched him so hard that the blood flowed out of his nose. He was in shock to find that this little, fiery girl gave him a bloody nose.

She was talented with children, gardening, and wanted to be a nurse. Her pastries and all that she baked were unique and delicious. Flowers and plants thrived under her gentle care. Her son Matthew acquired this talent from his mother. She was also a great dancer, and always dressed beautifully. She was a gentle spirit, and had many of Mama's qualities, especially with children. Anna married Ronald Izzo, son of Marina Vescuso [Mary] and Giovacchino [Jack Izzo]. Ronald had one sister, Angela. He and Anna were high school sweethearts.

Ronnie knew my husband Ralph before I knew him. They were close friends. The four of us spent many evenings dancing at Ralph's friend, Snookie's club and, restaurant, Hart's Cafe.

When Ralph and Ronnie got together, there was much laughter, as they recounted many of their former day experiences. Snookie would sit with us, and the three men would tell many tales. Occasionally, we would go to a neighborhood restaurant and lounge, The Meshanticut Green.

The families of my sisters and brothers did many things together. We spent many holidays together, celebrated each person's birthday, and loved and cared for each other. Our children loved their aunts and were secure with them, their uncles, and cousins. If one of the children needed discipline because they did something wrong, we would not hesitate to correct them. Cosmo and Aldo always imparted wisdom, direction, and love to our children.

It was sad that Anna and Ronnie passed within one year of the other. They were the parents of five children: Ronald Jr., Robert, Deborah, Stephen, and Matthew. Ronald is a successful attorney and has a law firm, Robert is headmaster at a prestigious school in Connecticut, Deborah is a nutritionist, Stephen is co-director of a well-known newspaper, and Matthew has a landscaping and design business and is in real estate investing.

Ronald, Stephen, Robert, Deborah, and Matthew Izzo

Janet and Robert Izzo family: Michael, Christopher, Ali

Nate and Jackson Izzo

The Izzo and Ostrowski families
Samuels graduation

Thomas Izzo, Stephen's son

One of my last memories of Anna was during one of my hospital visits with her. Anna was diagnosed with bladder cancer and was paralyzed from the waist down. She said, "Bert, I want you to make spaghetti and take it here. I want you to take china, crystal, silver, and a white tablecloth. When our friend Joanne comes to visit me, you will serve her." I did as she asked. I couldn't help thinking that this might have been the first time a sick patient asked for lunch to be served with the utmost class, for a faithful friend. Anna was the epitome of class. She was happy when she saw the table draped with fine white linen, flowers, silver, and homemade Italian food. I can say that I was touched by her thinking of someone else instead of herself, during excruciating circumstances. It was her way of thanking Joanne for being a faithful friend to her, over many difficult years. Anna passed on July 15, 2005.

I admire the closeness of their family. I couldn't help thinking their family is a tremendous tribute to Anna and Ronnie, the love they had shared, and the love that each of their children have for each other. Debbie reminds me of her mother. She is the strength of her family. What I and others see is the total dedication of each child to the other. What better gift or tribute could they give to their parents than the love and dedication they have for each other.

Marie married Mourad [James] Vartanian, son of Krishime Hahigian and Daka Vartanian and brother to two sisters, Lucy and Oski. Marie is creative in every aspect, especially in decorating, and sewing. She has great accounting skills and loves to entertain. When she was a teenager, she worked with Cozy Cardi, who was a well-known seamstress and decorator. She has made many beautiful designer dresses for Anna and me without using a pattern. There isn't anything she can't sew. Marie is knowledgeable and strongly believes in alternative medicine.

Jimmie was special to all of us. He had a way of making his nieces and nephews laugh and feel good about themselves.

Jim loved his wife Marie from the moment he saw her. He was affectionate to her, their family, and to our children.

Marie Capotosto Vartanian and Mourad Vartanian

Maria Giannini, Jim, Maria, James Vartanian

Mama (C) James, Judy, Marie, Jim Vartanian, Maria and Victor Giannini

Nicholas, James, Michael, Christopher, Kristiana,
Matthew. Giannini, and Vartanian cousins

His pride and joy were his children James and Maria and grand-children: Kristiana Giannini (a pharmacist) Michael Giannini (medical research), Nicholas Giannini (cybersecurity), James Vartanian (mechanical engineer and military), his brothers Christopher (criminal justice and military), and Matthew (first-year college student). He freely expressed the great pride he had for his son James Vartanian, an accomplished, retired army Colonel. He had a connection and love for Maria that only a father and daughter share. He nicknamed her "Mario" and would laugh heartily when he referred to his Mario. Maria has a God-given gift with training animals and is a professional photographer. He loved working in his yard and took great pride in its beauty. Jim passed on July 11, 2014. After years of sorrow over the early death of Jimmy's wife Judith, he would have been overjoyed that his son Jimmy had recently married Christine Hall.

Cosmo, the youngest, was born during a February1945, winter blizzard. Mama had a difficult pregnancy and delivery. Our brothers, Aldo and Luke, would sneak Papa's van and drive to St. Joseph's Hospital in Providence to visit her, bringing food and baked goods. Fifteen-year old, Luke, did not have a license to drive. Only by the grace of God did they get home safely.

Mama gave me instructions as she lay in bed. She would tell me what to do for the baby, how to change, wash, hold, and feed him. Aldo and I took care of his every need. We called him "Mucci." We were protective of the baby and made sure he wanted for nothing. My brothers and sisters, and I spoiled him. He brought much joy to our family.

None of us were spoiled by Papa, but Cosmo was. If he wanted a funny book during the night, Papa would pretend to go to Marty's Spa, just to prove to his son that the store was not open. Cosmo attended Northeastern University and the University of Rhode Island. He graduated with a degree in business. He is brilliant, creative with inventions, and would daily try to tease all of us with riddles. Being the youngest, he would want to be part of everything we did. He often threatened to tell Papa that my sisters and I were talking with boys during the feast of the Madonna della Civita if we wouldn't allow him to go to the feast with us. Of course, he always won. We did not want Papa to know we talked with boys. Our father was strict and protective. Cosmo was loved beyond words. He loved Mama and Aldo and took care of them throughout their lives.

Cosmo with our dog Brownie

Cosmo Alphonse Blaise Capotosto

When Ralph Jr., wanted to go to culinary school, I was against it. I kept asking him, "What happened to your goal of becoming a district attorney?" Cosmo offered to take us to the Culinary Institute of America in Hyde Park, New York, so Ralph would be able to judge more clearly if this was the direction he wanted to pursue. When we arrived at the institute and began to tour it, I was amazed at the creativity of the students, and all they produced. I looked at the profession with a more open mind. Ralph did end up studying culinary arts for a year at Johnson and Wales, when it first opened in Providence, staffed by members of the Culinary Institute. He spent several years studying in Italy.

As teenagers, each of us was included in our activities, especially when our brothers drove to Olivo's or Scarborough beaches on Sundays. We all gathered in Luke's car, and couldn't wait to feel the warm breeze, lie in the hot sand, and experience the view of the ocean. We climbed the rocks; the boys went fishing, and the girls would later go to the beach with firm instructions to meet at Luke's car at a certain time. God forbid if we were late arriving at the car.

After our marriages and we began having children, my sisters and I had our family gatherings at Olivo's Beach each Sunday, during the summers with our children. Mama would come with us, as she watched her grandchildren make sandcastles, play games, and run into the water with their cousins. They loved the water and were continually under the watchful eyes of their parents. The food was endless. Macaroni never tasted so good as when we ate it at the beach. Our husbands would grill hotdogs, steak, hamburgers, or whatever we brought. The children loved the watermelon, pastries, toasted marshmallows, and all of the other goodies we brought with us. We made sure there was enough food to last the day into night. Our children were brought up as if they were sisters and brothers, and to this day have close bonds and love for each other. Those years were the best of our lives.

Mama making pizza dough with daughter Bernadette

CHAPTER 10
THE GAETANINA AND GAETANA WAY

We heated the house with coal and later a Glenwood oil stove. Papa taught me how to make gravy. The stovetop was scorching hot. With Papa's help, I would place the large pots of gravy and soup on the stovetop, as they simmered for hours. Papa encouraged me and complimented me on whatever I made. Mama gave me instructions as she lay in bed.

Making gravy (we called it gravy then, although it is traditionally called sauce now) was a project in earlier days. Mama started the base with oil, lard, or cotenne (pig's skin). She made endless meatballs and added them to the gravy. Other meat options were braciole, sausage, and a piece of beef that was added to the gravy. To each can or jar of pre-served tomatoes, we would add one can of tomato paste, with an equal amount of water, and fresh herbs. Garlic sautéed in oil, until it became translucent, was always the start. The gravy simmered for hours until it was thick. If it was too thick, we would add small amounts of water. We also added herbs such as basil, parsley, salt, and pepper to enhance the taste. Other choices if one desired, were oregano and hot pepper seeds. Even though we were poor, and daily life was difficult, we always man-aged to eat well. Everything was cooked from scratch, and nothing was wasted. Mama prepared the simplest things as if it were gourmet food. She had an extraordinary gift of seasoning foods and making something ad niente (out of nothing). My son, Ralph, inherited this remarkable gift.

I loved walking into our home after attending the ten o'clock Mass at St. Mary's Church in Cranston and singing in our church choir on Sunday mornings. I began singing in the church choir when I was fif-teen years of age. My sisters and I would go to church together, and the boys went separately. At times, my brothers were altar boys. Mama, usu-ally went to a different Mass other than the one her children attended, so she would have time to cook a complete Sunday dinner. Papa didn't attend Mass regularly.

Our home was old, and drafty, but always spotless. The three bed-rooms were off the kitchen. My sisters and I shared a room, Luke, Aldo and Cosmo shared another room. Mama and Papa had their own bed-room with beautiful mahogany furniture. The bathroom was in a separate area behind our kitchen, next to our living room, and was extremely cold in the winter. Mama changed the curtains for the windows frequently. As we entered the door into our home, the stove was facing us. Our large white porcelain table was usually draped with a white tablecloth. Mama would be standing at our Barstow stove, frying potato croquettes, stirring the gravy, and checking the large cake or pie in the oven made without a written recipe. I would be famished after Mass, and quickly break a piece of Italian bread off a freshly baked loaf and dip it into the gravy, eat a meatball that was just fried, and impatiently wait for all of it to be served.

Listening to Antonio Pace's Italian radio show was a ritual on Sunday mornings for Mama and Papa. It was their soap opera time. Mama continued cooking as they listened and commented in Italian. On Sunday afternoons, our multiple course dinners would last for hours. There was no such thing as rushing or insisting that we had someplace to go to with our friends. Family dinners were a priority, and nothing stood in the way. Mama would serve us as if we were royalty.

She spoiled all of her children, making the foods they liked. During the week, she made spaghetti or linguini fini for Papa and me, and mezzani, or mezza ziti for the others. Sundays she usually cooked ziti, rigatoni, mezzani, or a special pasta such as Schiaffoni, manicotti, ravioli, or lasagna. We made cavatti with a machine that Papa sold. Potato gnocchi was a longer process. The dough was rolled into rope-like strips and cut into small pieces. We pressed and rolled the center of each piece with our finger, or over a fork. Homemade fettuccini was always a favorite. Mama would place a clean white sheet on her bed, and she gently spread the freshly made fettuccini on the sheet, until she was ready to cook it. If someone asked for a special food, she would cook their choice, as she did when making uovo in Purgatorio for Papa.

Each year, Papa would plant a large garden under the pear tree, beside the tenants' parking spots. At the end of the summer, Mama and Papa would preserve tomatoes, tomato paste, and many other vegetables for the winter. We pickled multiple jars of eggplant, and a mixture of green peppers, onions, cauliflower, and carrots. A delicious antipasto was made for the holidays and Sundays with this giardiniera. We picked grapes from our grapevines, and preserved grape jam sealed with wax, for our snacks. Herbs and hot peppers were dried and stored for the winter. All of our meals were made from scratch, with fresh foods and preserves. We learned how to do everything, especially knowing how to survive when times became difficult.

The hot dishes Mama made were the best. Escarole (Scarola) and beans, Pasta e Fagioli (pasta fazool), Pasta e Patata, Pasta e Ceci, minestrone, the soup she made with all of the fresh vegetables from our garden, minestra, made with a prosciutto bone, plain or with freshly cooked cannellini beans, chicken, beef, stews, and lentil soups. When Mama had a pot of chicken soup simmering on the back burner of the stove, we would ladle the broth into a bowl, adding broken pieces of hard Italian bread. It was soothing, especially when we slurped the remainder of the broth in our cups or bowls. A delicate slap would tell us to stop the slurping. In a firm tone, we heard Mama say, "Have manners." We loved bread and beans, string beans, and potatoes, with a vinegar or lemon dressing and herb mixture, or with a light fresh tomato sauce. A favorite summer snack was slices of Italian bread topped with a salad of fresh garden tomatoes, onions, the delicate leaves of the inside of celery, olive oil, basil, and salt. *Broccoli rabe* was a favorite vegetable.

Our Cardi cousins lived in the apartments above the drug store. Cousins and kids who lived in Cardi's yard played together. Tony and Stephen loved Mama's chamarugas (snails). Toothpicks were used to extract the snail from its shell. It is still the topic of conversation among us. Fridays and Wednesdays were fast days in our home; meat was not eaten. Mama usually made one of her specialties, such as snails, merluzzo, whiting, or some other kind of fish. At times, we would have bread and beans. One of my favorite meals was fresh crabs or littlenecks in a light red sauce, over spaghetti. Whatever course she made was delicious. One night when we were eating crab, Marie choked on the shell. It was traumatic as Mama and Papa desperately tried to get the shell out of her throat. She has never eaten a crab since.

The peasant Neapolitan style food that the Italian immigrants cooked was unique, delicious, fresh, and simple. The salad was eaten at the end of our meal. If leftover salad remained on the table, I would eat it, and Mama would tease me, saying, "You are a walking garbage pail."

Our preserved pickled peppers, marinated eggplant (melanzane), cured fresh olives, Italian bread, and cheese were a staple in our home. Whatever Mama preserved was considered a treat during the winter months. On Sunday nights our table would be set with antipasto, cold cuts, leftover meat, and meatballs from our Sunday dinner, macaroni, and other foods, in case anyone wanted a sandwich, or simply to make a dish (an expression we used when placing food in a dish). Following in her grandmother Gaetana's customs, Mama always seemed to be feeding many people who visited each Sunday.

Our daily school lunches were the envy of many classmates in Jr. High School and High School. Mama's culinary creativity seemed to have no end. She made me spinach and eggs, peppers and eggs, Italian tuna, salami (one of the few meat items I would eat) with mustard, lettuce and tomatoes, meatballs for my brothers, broccoli rabe greens, and eggplant. The lunch bags were stained with oil. Schoolmates would try to entice me and other classmates to exchange lunches. They would be sick of eating baloney or peanut butter and jelly sandwiches.

Eating dinner was a time for quiet and gratitude for all that was given to us. Whatever Mama cooked or baked was blessed by her when she made the sign of the cross and sprinkled holy water over her family and the food she was about to serve. Papa would always start by saying to us, "Manga, beva, e sta' zitto." (Eat, drink, and be quiet). Our father drank wine with dinner. After dinner, our parents had a demitasse cup of black coffee (espresso), with a bit of anisette or Sambuca. On occasion, it was served as an aperitif, when guests visited. Brandy was available if someone was ill with the flu. Often, a small amount was mixed in hot tea. Specialty cordials were other options available for guests. Our parents never feared their children tapping into the liquor bottles which were stored in a cabinet. Our family were not drinkers. While eating dinner on Sundays, Mama would give us a small amount of wine mixed with orange soda (orangata). It, was a treat, as was drinking sarsaparilla, orange, Moxie, or cream soda. Golden ginger ale was available, especially if one of us had an upset stomach or was sick.

Cleaning up after the big dinners was hard. Mama liked using clean white dishes for every course. We had piles of dishes, glasses, pots, pans, and utensils that were washed in scorching-hot water so that the dishes would be sterilized. If I complained that my hands were burning, she would tell me the water had to be hot enough to kill the germs. We did not have hot water or a dishwasher, so the water we used for washing dishes, clothes, or taking baths had to be boiled.

It seemed that everything we were given to eat was either a treat or for medicinal purposes. Chamomile was freshly picked in the fields and made into a tea for stomach ailments. Often, we would pick dandelion from the fields and Mama would cook the greens or make a fresh salad with it. Dandelion was considered very healthy. The elders believed it contained abundant iron and other nutrients and was good for one's liver. It was either sautéed with garlic and olive oil and served as a vegetable or cut up and used in a salad. Tea can also be brewed with the dandelion. The elders used everything available and knew how to cook them. To this day, I still love dandelion.

In the household, Mama believed the girls should care for the needs of the boys in the family, as she was taught in Italy. I never knew why Mama didn't sit down to eat with us. I would often ask her, "Ma, why aren't you eating with us?" She would smile and say with much love, "In a while, I want to serve my family first." It wasn't until I became older and wiser than I realized she would eat the leftovers. She made sure there was enough food for all of us. Sometimes, I saw her eating a piece of bread, dunking it into a cup of black coffee. She did it without complaint, and with an abundance of love.

Walking by Marty's Spa and peering into the large storefront window each day, brought us many temptations. Each of us had a sweet tooth for the Yankee Doodles, Devil Dogs, Ring Dings, and the small pies that lined the front window of Marty's. Walking by the store and peering in their front window, our mouths would water, as we were deciding on what Table Talk pie we wanted if we had ten cents to buy one. Funny books, song sheets, potato chips, a piece of candy (squirrel nuts were a favorite) or bubble gumballs were always temptations. My sisters and I would paint our lips red, with a bright red gumball, pretending it was lipstick, as we walked around the neighborhood. We hoped our father would not notice when we returned home. Even though we rubbed the red off our lips, thinking our secret was safe, Papa always knew what we had done when we walked into the house. In no uncertain terms, he told us to wash the red off our lips.

Katherine and Ralph listening to Enrico's stories

CHAPTER 11
THE STORYTELLERS

I admired the storytellers in our daily lives. My generation learned much from them. Mama was our main storyteller. After eating Sunday dinner, she would take a brief rest. Her daughters would lie down on the bed with her. It was her storytime. She loved telling us stories of events that her grandparents experienced. Mama explained, "Grandma would make lots of pizza. It was so good. She never knew who would come to her door in need of food. She was always prepared."

She continued, "One day, Grandma opened her door to a knock. A tall, bearded man stood at her door. He was carrying a staff and was wearing a long brown garment. The man told Grandma he was hungry and thirsty. She invited him to come in saying, "I made pizza, eat, and have something to drink." Gaetana gave the man a container filled with pizza. She asked the stranger if he had any other needs. The man blessed her and said, "I came because I know you love God, serve the poor, and make good pizza. God knows all the good you do. He knows how much food and pizza you make and how you take care of the needy. He blesses you." He blessed her and walked out the door.

Mama exclaimed, "There was something different about this man. He told grandma that he knew all she had done for the poor, the homeless, the blind, and the sick."

With joy she said, "Grandma immediately went to the door, to see where he went. She couldn't see him. She asked others if they saw him. They told her, "No, we never saw him at all." His coming and going were a mystery. Grandma said, "He looked like St. Joseph, and she believed that God sent him to her house." Grandma continued to describe him, saying, "He had piercing eyes, was very gentle and kind, and was different from anyone who had ever entered our home. His coming and going were mysterious. He came from nowhere and left unseen by anyone else."

Remembering every detail, she told us that her grandparents converted several garages, attached to their house, and made it into a hostel for pilgrims and the needy. Her grandmother washed the feet of the pilgrims, fed, clothed, and allowed them to sleep there. Mama continued by saying, "They helped the blind. Often, blind people would come to our hostel. If anyone needed shoes, and grandma didn't have any, she would take her shoes off and give them to whoever needed them." It seemed as if her work was endless and selfless.

Mama's stories were vivid and real. I believed each one and was intrigued by them. I was told that Mama didn't have it easy in Italy; she worked hard, and her grandmother was a tough, determined, strict woman, who gave her life to help others, hosting dinners for the clergy, hierarchy in the Catholic church, guests, and feeding the needy. She needed her granddaughters help for the never-ending daily chores. In former days, it seemed that parents were not as hard on boys as they were on girls. The women were expected to serve the men, and care for their daily needs. I'm sure if we were to interview the men in our family, they would tell us a different version.

Another well-known and cherished story was when I was three years of age, a man came to her door and asked for money. Mama had fifty cents to her name. She gave it to him and asked what his name was. A day later, I was run over by one of Uncle Alfred's construction workers, Julius. Mama and the women who lived in the Cardi apartments were sitting outside in front of Mary and Steve Palumbo's apartment. They were watching their children while they played. Excited to see Papa's car pull into his parking spot, I ran to meet him. The car, which was heading for the garage, ran over me. I was told that the tires went over my body. Those who had witnessed the accident were hysterical, thinking I was dead. Except for a miracle, there wasn't any way I could be alive. To everyone's surprise, crying and in a state of terror, I somehow got up and walked. My only memory was walking daily with our cousin Anna Migliori Ferri, who was six months older than me, with heavily bandaged legs, from our tenement house to the A. Cardi Construction Co. garage. Family and neighbors exclaimed, "It is a miracle that you lived." Luke vividly remembers the incident.

That night, Mama had a dream of a man holding a diaper in his hand. Within the diaper was a fifty-cent piece. He said, "My name is Peter; because of the fifty cents you gave to me, your daughter lived." Mama told Papa of the dream and described the man named Peter. Papa explained, "I know who he is. He is the father of my close friend from Itri. I sent money to my friend to help pay for medical expenses when his father Peter was ill and dying."

Each feast day of St. Peter and Paul on June 29, Mama would call me early in the morning and say, "It's the feast of St. Peter and Paul, did you go to Mass to say thank you?" I would always laugh because she didn't miss a beat. She remembered everything.

I would answer, "Yes, Ma, I'll be going to Mass." That was her life, always thanking God for everything. She didn't throw a crumb of bread away without offering it up to Jesus for the souls in purgatory. She explained, "When my father had problems that seemed insurmountable to solve, he would offer up everything to the souls in purgatory. She continued, "Papa always received the help he needed."

Mama moved to Oaklawn in the early1960s after the Cardi property was sold. She would take long daily walks. Many younger people who knew her from Knightsville, would offer her a ride home, and the wife of a local official would stop to offer her a ride in her limousine. Vendors would come out to greet her, and the local florist would give her flowers or a rose. People loved her. Often, the younger generation whose families came from Itri sought out her knowledge about their ancestors and family roots. She would tell them many important details and stories about their families. They were fascinated and mesmerized by the knowledge she had of their relatives.

Wanting to repay a kindness that was shown to her, she would insist on buying coffee, lunch, or pizza for the person who offered her a ride home. Like her grandparents, Mama did not care if she had five cents, one dollar, or didn't know if she would have anything the next day for her own needs. If someone was in need, she would freely give away whatever she had. No one could stop her; many tried.

St. Mary's Church

CHAPTER 12
LIVING IN KNIGHTSVILLE

We thought we had it tough growing up. When I think back, I realize how fortunate we were to grow up with tremendous love from family and community, with morals, spirituality, and always being involved in our church. Everything for our parents was based on trusting in God and believing He would always provide for and protect us if we honored Him. We believed in miracles, prayed the rosary, lit candles in front of a statue of Our Lady, or one of our favorite saints, believing that our needs and prayers would be answered. Family (all of our relatives) and church were the center of our lives. Attending the Lenten mission was expected of us, as the priest preached a fire and brimstone message, placing the fear of God in us.

In our youth, life was simpler when we lived in Knightsville. Many people were related and knew each family because most of them were Italian immigrants from Itri, Italy. We walked everywhere. St. Mary's Church was our parish and community. The priests knew all of the families and children personally and made no bones about reprimanding us. Our religion and faith were essential, and our pastor Father Schettini taught us well. He gave the youth and parishioners direction and spiritually and led his people by example. One of his famous quotes was, "A parish without prayer is cold and sterile despite the beautiful buildings it may have." (Conte 2014) He was a man for his people and a man of God. Father Schettini was a close friend of Grandpa Cardi, and after our grandfather's death remained close to his family. He and Grandpa Cardi, along with Luigi Merluzzo and Luigi Vallone were the founders of St. Mary's Church. Grandpa Cardi was the initiator of the cause for the Itrani people, to have their Italian church. They refused to tolerate the continual disrespect and lack of opportunities for their families and the Italian community. They fought for their children to be educated and for them to able to practice their faith freely.

Rev. Cesare Schettini

Dedication of St. Mary's Church. Conte: 2014

I'm sad for Millennials and Gen Z'ers who have not experienced that kind of faith and family commitments. During my childhood, there was not any extreme liberalism. We had rules, and we followed them, like it or not. We wouldn't dare defy our parents or elders with disobedience or disrespect. God forbid if we ever dared to walk by an elder without respectfully greeting them.

Our every move was scrutinized, and the girls were watched closely. We were told in no uncertain terms if our actions, and how we dressed, gave a negative impression or message.

Anna Migliori (cousin) and I were would laugh endlessly at the mischievous things we attempted. Of course, we never got away with anything. Our parents, as well as Uncles Alfred, Americo, and Auntie Angie would usually be aware of what we were up to. Neighborhood men gathered each day in front of Marty's Spa or Medical Arts Pharmacy (Cardi's) on Cranston Street. They kept an eye on every kid in the neighborhood. If one of us did something wrong in their eyes, it would be reported to our father, and we would hear about it.

Mama walked with her children to the cemetery to visit the graves of family members and friends. She instilled this practice in us. When I became an adult, she would give me strict orders as to what color and kind of flowers to place at each gravesite. She would emphatically say,

"And don't forget Father Schettini." Marie and I maintain this practice, to the present time.

If one of us had whooping cough, Mama would walk with us to the closest farm, usually the Del Bonis farm on Phenix Avenue, to breathe in the smell of manure. She would tell us, "Breathe deeply, manure heals the whooping cough." Their natural remedies were endless, and most of the time accomplished the needed healing.

During WWII, many families did not know how they would cloth or feed their families. Mothers would stand in line for hours at the Brick Store on Cranston Street, beyond the Cranston Print Works, to obtain flour, sugar, and other necessities (whatever they were given). S&H Green Stamps were given out, and parents used them to shop for food. The women cooked everything from scratch and relied upon their preserves for the long, hard, cold, winter months. We often wore hand-me-downs. Everything in moderation was the theme of that period. Nothing was wasted. Recycling was not a new invention for people in that era.

We walked daily, to Soprano's market. Spirito's, Marino's, Fabrizio's markets were other options. We went to Cardi's drug store daily for medical needs. Buying an ice-cream cone was a treat. Oftentimes we would go to Soprano's several times a day because Mama would need something. Shopping was done daily. Comare and Compare Soprano recorded the amount of what was purchased in a book. At the end of the week, Mama would pay them. This procedure was offered to many of the Italian immigrants who shopped in local stores. The city hall and police station were located at the corner of Cranston Street and Phenix Avenue (the gazebo was built on that site). We walked everywhere. When Cardi's Furniture was established, people would be able to pay their utility bills there.

We walked each day to Knightsville School, Highland Park School, Bain Junior High School, or Cranston High School, in the heat, rain, blizzards, and snow. If by chance we had ten cents to take the bus, which was not often, we were treated badly by non-Italians from Meshanticut and Oaklawn. They called us "the farmers," or "the wops," and we were expected to sit at the back of the bus. Discrimination was not foreign to the Italian culture. Being a child of an Italian immigrant, who spoke broken English, Luke, being the first-born child in our family, was often called, "The greenhorn." The non-Italians were bold and felt superior to us, but we ignored them as best we could.

There was much joy in our family when our brothers Aldo and Luke returned home from Germany after the Korean War. Our mother and family prayed night and day for their safety. We were excited when Luke and Aldo bought their first car. They treated us to steak sandwiches at Ted's Big Boy, Miss Cranston Diner, or Jolly Charlies.

The Cardi Farm

We would wait with great expectation for Uncle Rico to pick us up on Sunday mornings to take us to his camp, "The Farm." He would make his usual stops at Miss Cranston Diner, or Jolly Cholly's, and a local market to buy food and treats, before driving to the camp. Uncle Rico would cook up a storm for family and friends, and whatever he cooked was delicious. We were thrilled to be there with our aunts, uncles, and cousins. It was a treat for us to be able to leave Cardi's yard.

During one of our Sunday visits to the camp, Uncle Rico warned Luke not to roam far into the woods to hunt. Somehow, he wandered and could not find his way back. Uncle Rico was worried and furious when darkness approached. He was mainly frightened for Luke's safety. He called the state police to look for him. Luke explained, "I kept circling the camp, but did not know it." When Luke entered the camp, Uncle Rico was relieved beyond words. He expressed his relief and anger by flinging a frying pan at him. Of course, it missed Luke. This story is still told today by our cousins.

Our mother's and relatives usually sort out the medical knowledge of Uncle Alfred Cardi. If one of us was injured, Uncle Alfred, a pharmacist, would clean and bandage our wounds. He was the elder brother of Uncle Rico, and their wives were sisters. The brothers had close relationships with their sisters and their children. It seemed they were usually up to date on all the activities of their nieces and nephews. They made no bones about telling us if we were on the wrong path in their eyes. Our mothers loved it, and never interfered if we were corrected by our aunts and uncles. We still maintain our relationships with most of our relatives.

Mama and Papa encouraged each of us to use our talents. Mama did not care what kind of mess we made. She would say with joy, "A mess can always be cleaned." We lived in an atmosphere where our talents grew. We did not have a television or a telephone, until years later when we became teenagers. We would listen to radio programs such as Inner Sanctum Mystery, Fibber Mc Gee and Molly, Family Theatre, The Lawrence Welk Show, and Only the Shadow Knows. When we finally were able to obtain a small black and white Philips Television, we were glued to the screen as we watched The Lone Ranger and Tonto, Roy Rogers, and his horse Trigger, and Dale Evans, The Ed Sullivan Show, Milton Berle, Howdy Doody, Arthur Godfrey, I Love Lucy, Gunsmoke, Lassie, The Three Stooges, Philco Television Playhouse, Kraft Theater, along with other programs our parents approved of. We watched in wonder as Ed Sullivan introduced Elvis Presley and the Beatles. In reverence, we sat quietly when Kate Smith sang the National Anthem and God Bless America. Before some of us were teens, my brothers grilled sandwich steaks using a hand grill. They held the grill over the hot coals in our stove. Our Saturday ritual was eating delicious steak sandwiches for lunch, when and if our parents were able to afford to buy thinly cut sandwich steak, for all of us. Aldo loved sprinkling vinegar on his steak. He would say, "You don't know what you're missing."

Later, on Saturday afternoons, Papa would insist we listen to The Metropolitan Opera on the radio. He knew all of the operas well. He would passionately explain each of them to us as we gathered around our small radio. Papa would tell us to be silent as we waited for our cousin Lucy Cardi, to sing The Indian Love Call Song on a local talent radio show early Sunday afternoon, as our family sat at the dinner table. He was proud of her talent, and we were happy to hear her sing. Music was part of his soul and encompassed our home.

I distinctly remember when Papa started his own import-export business. In a corner of our kitchen, on a small colonial mahogany table, he decoratively placed his first arrival of spaghetti bowls from Italy, with the name of his company imprinted on the bottom of each bowl. He was proud.

Shortly after Papa started his business, and it began to grow, he rented the storefront in the house we lived in, at 1707 Cranston Street. He imported demitasse coffee pots, macaroni machines, ravioli forms, cavatti makers, machines to make strata (tomato paste), cheese graters, and many other household items. He had an array of dishes, dinnerware, glasses, cups and saucers, Italian pottery, and a selection of other articles.

In the late 40s or early 1950s, the store was the retail portion of the business. Each day he went to businesses throughout Rhode Island to sell his merchandise wholesale. Shepard's Department Store, the Outlet Company, hardware stores, and well-known gift stores in Silver Lake, Federal Hill, and throughout Rhode Island were some of his clientele.

To this day, many beautiful crystal glasses, spaghetti bowls, fine china, demitasse coffee pots, statues, and cups and saucers, and pottery he imported from Italy, and other countries, remain in the china closets of many homes. He was the first in Rhode Island to sell espresso coffee makers. As I was writing this book, an acquaintance from Knightsville approached me smiling. She said, "I still have a spaghetti bowl with the name of your father's store stamped on the bottom. I treasure it and display it on a shelf in our kitchen."

Mama was notorious for giving away the store. She would take things off the shelf, giving it to someone she thought needed it. Sustaining the loss never entered her mind. Although it may have bothered Papa, we never heard about it.

I often think of Mama when I open my cupboards. Papa had given me sets of different-size crystal stemware before my wedding in 1956. He also made sure I had spaghetti bowls, linens, demitasse coffee makers, and whatever else he had to sell. One day, after Ralph and I moved into our home, Mama came to my house and walked to my cupboard. She looked at me and said, "Betta, the nuns at St. Mary's just moved into their convent, they need everything. I'm taking these (stemware, bowls, cups, and saucers, etc.). I'll give them back to you." Knowing they would never be replaced, I argued, "Ma, Papa gave those to me. I want to keep them." She ignored me and went on to do her thing. That was Mama. God will provide, just give what you have.

Papa's nephews Eddie, Bobbie, and Paul came to our home often to learn whatever they could about the import and export business. With Papa's guidance, they became very successful in New York City. Papa was admired by his family and looked upon him as a man who had the foresight and courage to follow his inspirations, in a time when things were hard, especially when one walked alone with little money and a family of eight to feed. I admired him tremendously, and now that I am older and understand more clearly, I am sorry I didn't follow in his footsteps, as he wanted me to.

Papa reinventing his career

JUNE 1937

Cardi's yard tenants:
Capotosto, Cardi, Ciccione, Migliori, Pallotta, Palumbo,
Paolino, and Piacneti

CHAPTER 13
GROWING UP

As the years began to pass from childhood to adulthood, each of us had different roles in our family. Mama would often say, "You can have twenty children, and they will be different." I believe that we cannot be placed in another person's mold and love with the capacity that was given to us alone. Our thinking, needs, and life stories are unique and different from anyone else's.

We grew up in a time when most of us were poor. We had little to nothing of material possessions. Our parents encouraged us to make whatever we needed. I vividly remember when I was in first or second grade, Aldo and Luke wrapped and made a large ball of thin tin foil from cigarette wrappings, to sell to the ragman Mr. Frank La Polla as he bellowed, "rags, rags," throughout the streets. They intended to buy my first pair of boots with the money they made. It is a memory that I will never forget. They had a goal and accomplished it with great love so that I would have the needed boots. That was how our family was. We did anything to help each other.

If the soles of our shoes had holes in them, they were not discarded, we made cardboard soles until we could have them repaired by John Scardera, the local shoemaker. When Papa was still living and we were in our early years, before our teens, Mama would pack our Sunday dinner and we would all climb into Papa's Model T Ford to go to the reservoir. Papa would find a spot with a picnic table, and we would eat our Sunday dinner there. Often, we had trouble with the car and had to wait patiently until Papa and Luke fixed it. In the summer, Papa would take us, and one of our close friends to Oakland Beach, and we would take turns lying on his back, and holding him tightly as he swam.

Most of the kids in our neighborhood attended Knightsville School. If we came home and complained about a teacher who disciplined us, our parents would never go against a teacher; they would add more discipline or punishment. Respect for our elders was not a questionable matter. It was expected. In the Italian families, grandparents were respected and cared for by their families.

Children who emigrated from Italy sent money to their impoverished parents or family members, helping them to survive, even though they had little for themselves.

John Scardera, Providence Journal

Our community would celebrate children's talents by having talent shows, usually held at Highland Park School. We couldn't wait to see who the winners would be. My brothers and I would win first prize in the musical division. Luke and Aldo would make their musical instruments using a washboard, a metal tub for drums, or pots, pans, and a harmonica. I would tap dance and sing or have a lead part in a play (usually Cinderella or the wicked witch). Mama would make beautiful costumes from lace curtains, and colorful fabric for the twins. They repeatedly won first prize during specific contests or other celebrations. She was talented in many ways.

Our tenement apartment seemed to be a haven for relatives and friends. Our home was usually filled with people. Mama and Papa had many relatives who visited often, and friends were always welcomed in our home. Papa's aunt, Innocenza, came to visit daily. Each Sunday afternoon she, her daughter-in-law Mary and Mary's children would visit our home. Our family loved her, and she was considered our grandma, that's what we called her. She often brought fresh lettuce and vegetables from her garden during the summer. She walked for miles daily and planted her garden until the end. She died at the age of 105. She and her children were family to each of us.

Anna and Marie Capotosto
First prize winners for most original costumes

Zia Innocenza Lorello Saccoccia

Our family, neighbors, relatives, and other friends joined us as we sang Neapolitan songs and danced to the music Papa played on his guitar. On a weekend night, or usually Saturday night or Sunday, he planned our get-togethers, and there was never any loss in participants. It was a happy time for all of us. Gathering under the pear tree was a common experience. It was our gathering place and special to all of us. Those of us who grew up in Cardi's yard knew well that the pear tree was our special place for us to gather or simply sit alone. Neighbors and relatives sat there in the summer months to try to keep cool from the summer heat, always with a watchful eye on the kids.

The women confided in one another, especially if there was hardship in one of the families. They talked about everything. Often one of us would sit there alone. I began writing poetry under the pear tree. Mostly, we looked forward to the nights that Papa played the guitar or mandolin so we could sing and dance. Uncle Rico would sit in his black Cadillac and watch as we had fun. Friends and former neighbors have little difficulty recapturing their childhood memories, especially those who lived in Cardi's yard. Meeting under the pear tree is unforgettable to most of us. The forbidden tree, as I call it was full of beautiful, delicious pears that we were not allowed to touch or eat. When we knew we were not being watched we sneakily picked the pears, savoring each bite.

Mama would give us five cents to buy ice cream at Uncle Alfred's drug store. Often, she would tell Arthur Pallotta (Tilliuch) to make coffee cabinets. She secretly gave him an egg or two and told him to add it to the mixture. She had many remedies for our strength and health. Giving us cod liver oil, each day was a must. When she began to have grandchildren, she gave them cod liver oil, as she did with her own children. My son, Ralph, still talks about Nonni giving him cod liver oil. I think if we were to ask each older grandchild, they too would remember the spoons of cod liver oil given to them.

Many of the elders used beaten egg whites to heal fractured bones or wounds. Children and adults with illnesses or injuries knew where and who to go to for treatment of their ailments.

The elders also knew who to see to have the evil eye (malocchio) removed from a family member. There were many superstitions. Children were scared to death the night lady would harm them. Many of our mothers visited a neighborhood friend named Mariucca who knew how to get rid of the evil eye. Mariucca would pour drops of oil into a bowl of water and pray in Italian. If the beads of oil separated, resembling an eye, it was thought the person had the evil eye. The sign of the cross was made repeatedly on the victim's forehead until the healer felt that the "malocchio" left them.

We were told not to drink anything ice cold, because it would harm our stomach. Most women carried scarves or shawls with them, for fear of getting a draft from the cold air. One never sat under a fan and avoided drafts of any kind. They did not want to catch a cold.

Mama had unending patience in making banana curls for my sisters and me. Our hair was straight, and we would often tell her, "I wish I had curly hair." She would wrap each section with rags, and excitedly we waited to see the finished product the following morning. After all, if Shirley Temple could have banana curls, so could we.

She washed our white dresses by hand or used a washboard. She loved to dress us in our freshly washed, starched, and ironed white clothing. She lovingly polished our white shoes, as she lined them up on the counter to dry. We never looked unclean or sloppy. Mama would tell the girls, "Buy simple, classy dresses. They never go out of style, and you can always dress them up, or give them a different look. Knightsville was a great Italian community to live in. We walked everywhere and were never alone. The elders watched us as if we were their own. The men, including Papa, would stand in front of Marty's Variety Spa. The Spa was owned by Concetta and Marty Purificato, on the Antonio Cardi property. Papa and the Itrani men met in front of the store to talk about the happenings in our town while keeping a watchful eye on each child. Nothing got past them.

Gaetanina, Maria Civita Capotosto Sinapi, Mariucca Del Bonis

Cosmo (Papa) and a friend in front of Marty's Spa

Concetta and Marty Purificato, Marty's Spa

If we were sick with the flu, Mama would spread Vicks on our chest, and wrap a clean, warm flannel cloth around us. She would heat bricks in the oven, wrap them in flannel, and place them under our feet to keep us warm, especially during the frigid winter months. If Mama thought one of her children needed a doctor, Dr. Abate would make a home visit. We did not have heat; the houses were old, drafty, and cold. The only heat we had was from the Barstow or Glenwood stoves.

We walked to local stores and bakeries such as De Cubellis Bakery, Garzilli's Bakery, and later Solitro's Bakery to shop for food, bread, pastries, and to purchase other needs of the day. Some of our clothing was purchased at Sinapi's dry goods store, next door to our house.

Mr. Robertson would come to our home each week to sell Mama clothes, sheets, towels, bedspreads, and many other needs. Each week, Mama would make a payment towards her purchases. This was how most families purchased their needs. At times, Papa would take us to Mr. Robertson's store on Empire Street in Providence to purchase winter coats. It was not unusual for us to wear hand-me-down coats or clothing from older siblings or relatives. I often wore Aldo's coats.

We waited in anticipation to hear and see the peddlers announce their arrival on Cranston Street. We purchased our fish from the fish man Clem Soscia. The milkman delivered milk in glass bottles, and fresh fruits and vegetables were bought from the peddler. Ice for the icebox was purchased from the ice man or at the ice barn. Our icebox was nothing more than a small white box. Little would fit inside. During the cold winters, Mama would store food in a small closet outside our door. When she made Jell-O, she would wrap the bowl, and place it on a shelf outdoors during the frigid winter months.

Mama's close friend, Maria Matrullo, a kind, wonderful woman, made the most fabulous Italian bread. Opening the door on a cold, below zero winter night after hearing a knock, one of Maria's daughters would be standing there holding a large, round-shaped bread that was piping hot.

Maria carefully wrapped the bread in a heavy blanket and sent us a large round loaf each time she baked the bread. Mama would slice the bread and pour extra virgin olive oil over the slices. That would be our snack. It was a poor man's snack, and one of our favorites. Some people sprinkled sugar on the oiled slices, but we liked ours plain.

De Pasquale Square outdoor market: Providence Historical Society

When I was 12-14 years of age, Papa would take me to Federal Hill to purchase fish, fruits, vegetables, and Italian delicacies from the line of peddlers on De Pasquale Square and Atwells Avenue, or in specialty stores.

When he went to New York for business, and to see relatives, he took back many delicacies that were difficult to find in stores at home. He knew exactly where to buy authentic New York cheesecake, and we waited patiently for him to return home so we could devour it.

We were fortunate to have great neighbors such as the Sinapis, Sopranos, and Frabrizios who lived in houses next door to Cardi's yard. The Ialongos, Maggiacomos, Churches, and Marinos lived across the street from us. The Saccoccio and Tamburino homes were next door to Medical Arts Pharmacy, and the Graziano Body Shop was next door to Cardi's Hardware.

Our families and our parents socialized with the community and tenants in Cardi's yard. They sat outside, usually under the pear tree or in front of Mary and Steve Palumbo's apartment. During the warm summer months, the mothers watched as their children communicated, played together, or had their spats. When a neighbor fought with us, Mama would always tell the other mother, "Don't get involved, let them work it out. We will be enemies, and they will soon be friends again."

Mary and Steve were Anna's (my sister) godparents and were special people in my life. Mary taught me how to pray the rosary. I spent a lot of time with her. She and Steve did not have any children. She treated both Victor Palumbo and me as if we were her children.

Bertha and Joseph Cicione were Marie's godparents, and their daughter, Louise, confirmed Marie. Louise was close to each of us and often took me to the theater in Providence. Following, we would go to Woolworth's for a sundae. After the theater one Saturday afternoon, Louise took me to Woolworth's.

She asked, "What kind of a sundae do you want?"

I thought for a moment, and quickly replied, "butterscotch sundae." After becoming sick from the sweetness, I never again had a butterscotch sundae.

Louise introduced me to roller skating rinks, which she frequented on Sunday afternoons. It was as if she were an older sister to me.

Mama would often invite the neighbors' children to our home, to have a snack with her homemade foods and baked goods. She would make trays of pancakes and biscotti for our friends and neighbors when we returned home from sledding on De Luca's hill, as she gleefully served us.

One of my fondest memories was when Papa would get up from our dinner table and dance with me. He wanted me to learn how to dance, and my siblings and I watched in amazement when he jived across our kitchen floor, dancing the Charleston. He was a fabulous dancer. His moves were smooth and fast. Anna and I acquired our love for dancing from him. Many of the elders who visited our home could not read or write. Our parents would read the letters they received from Itri. After discussions about the content, Mama would write a response for their relative or friend. We witnessed many of the elders' tears, as they felt a longing to see their families who lived in Itri. Our parents grieved with their friends and relatives who received news of a parent's or relative's death or illness. During WWII, and the bombing of Itri, most of the inhabitants of Itri ran to the hills looking for shelter. The enemies were ruthless, especially when they looked for young women to rape. Parents desperately looked for shelter away from town to protect their families. The men hid their wives and daughters. Papa's father Nonno Onorato died during the bombing of Itri, when he refused to leave his home.

Bernadette and Mary Palumbo

I can still picture Papa weeping, as he stood by the stove rubbing his hands when he received the news his father had died during the bombing of Itri.

Several years ago, I had a conversation with Pat Maggiacomo, an Italian immigrant who moved to Cranston when he came to America. He lived through the war in Itri. He described how families ran to the hills and found shelter in caves. He said, "At night, we would sneak out to find food in the fields or wherever we could, close to the caves. Their experience was terrifying, for the German soldiers were merciless." He continued, "Even though much of the town was destroyed, thank God, the American soldiers rescued the inhabitants of Itri."

Bombardment and rescue of Itri by American soldiers, 1944 (WWII archives) Conte: 2014

Luke's wife, Rita, often told our family of the horrors she and her family lived through in Caserta, Italy during the war. Emotionally, she told us how her mother would hide the girls in a space under their house so that the soldiers would not find them.

Being invited for the Aunt Jemima pancakes aunts Jeanette and Alene made for breakfast on Saturday mornings, was a treat. To this day, Luke still does lazupp (insuppare, dunking toast into his coffee) each morning for breakfast. When Mama would make hot cream of wheat or polenta, she would insist that we eat it saying, "It's good for you."

We played baseball, the old man with the shoe, jacks, fiddlesticks, hide and seek, tag, jump rope, jump the fence, hopscotch, kick the can, and many card games, especially knuckles. The games we played are too numerous to remember. It seemed that most kids loved to sing, and some were extremely talented in yodeling and harmonizing, especially one of the neighborhood kids, Tommy Cardillo.

We walked up the hill behind the A. Cardi Construction Co. garage, and the property our grandfather Antonio originally owned, to Knights-ville School each day. After his death, Grandpa's sons Alfred and Amer-ico inherited all of the property and businesses.

We walked to Knightsville, Highland Park, Hugh B. Bain Jr. High and Cranston High Schools in the rain, sleet, and snow. Each of us graduated high school. Papa would not hear of any of us not completing high school. Education was vitally important to him. He encouraged each of us to choose a profession, and would say, "Make something of yourself." He instilled in us, as our grandfather Antonio B. Cardi, firmly expressed to his children, "God, family, education and the United States of America are priorities and a privilege."

Our family and other tenants spent much time sitting under the pear tree. During the hot summer months, we found some relief from the hot sun, as we were protected by the tree. Many stories and memories can be told about our social life while sitting under the tree with our Sinapi, Cerrito, and Fusco relatives from New York, and their many visitors.

The only homes I was ever able to sleep at were the Miglioris or Sopranos. Aunt Annie's salami sandwiches were the best. The well, seasoned foods of the Sopranos were always good. Our mother and aunts were all great cooks. Aunts Angie and Anna made awesome sponge cakes, filled with homemade yellow cream, sprinkled lightly with confectioners' sugar. Mama was known for her delicious zeppole, pizza, and especially for her fried celery and cauliflower. Aunt Angie was well-known for her wedding and birthday cakes. She made cakes for many members of her family and relatives. It was always a treat tasting the cakes she made for our cousins when we attended their birthday parties. The wedding cakes were beautiful and any of her cakes were the best one would ever want.

Serving Mama and her sisters in the backyard of my home on a clear, warm, summer day was a joy for me. Their stories and love for each other were special. When their brother, Rico, surprised them with a visit, their faces lit up, and they would joyfully greet him crying out, "Rico." Their love for each other was evident. God forbid if anyone spoke negatively about their brother.

I would go to the docks at Galilee to purchase fresh crabs and lobsters. I have made crab that very same way many times during the summer, for Mama, my sister Anna, Virginia Soprano, friends, Tina Cardi, and Aunt Mary.

We have many success stories in our family tree. Successful businesses and professions exist with our relatives and members of our family.

I didn't realize how many published writers there were in our family background. Zio Vincenzo Capotosto was a published poet, who received the Presidential Award in Italy. Many of Mama's relatives were also writers, such as her uncles, Prof. Alfredo Cardi, Prof. Antonio Cardi, and cousin Prof. Mario Cardi. Several of the Capotosto relatives from New York, Raymond, and Eddie Sinapi worked in film. I don't find it coincidental that three of my grandchildren are writers. Kali, a student at Emerson College is a creative writer and interested in playwriting. Krishan who is still in high school is an athlete, writer, and artist. Raphael is a screenwriter. Rose and Stephen Cardi's daughter Annie is a published author, and two of the Migliori children are in film directing. Zoë has a degree from Full Sail University in film directing and photography.

Vincenzo Capotosto Article: (La Provincia)

Beatrice Marino, Bernadette, Sylvia Palumbo, Elena Marino

CHAPTER 14
CONTINUED FRIENDSHIPS

My friends and I loved to dance to the sound of big, name bands. We were in our late teens, and some in their early twenties. Port Arthur and the Arcadia ballrooms were popular places for dancing. Port Arthur was known to the sailors who came to town as a great place to dance, and to meet a young woman. I was not allowed to go to either place. I was close friends with Elena and Beatrice Marino and Sylvia Palumbo. Weekly we would go dancing at Rhodes on the Pawtuxet and to hear the music of big-name bands. When a friend's brother or a neighbor came home from the service after the Korean War, I along with Beatrice and Elena Marino would give them dance lessons in the Marino's living room. Many of the men met their current spouses at

Rhodes after we taught them to dance. Anthony Marino met his wife, Evelyn, the first night he went to Rhodes on the Pawtuxet.

Mary Marino Manzi, Mary, and Anna Carpentier, Beatrice Marino
Our weekly group at the Manzi and Darzio homes

Anthony and Mary (Marino) Manzi, Anthony's sister Theresa and her husband Manny Darzio welcomed us into their homes. We had much support, advice, and felt loved by many of the married couples and friends, who often guided us. We were invited to Mary and Anthony's tree-trimming party before Christmas, and the New Year's Eve parties they hosted.

Usually, the Carpenters and Scaralias would spend time in the Manzi home with all of us. A weekly Friday night ritual was visiting the home of Theresa. If we brought friends with us, everyone would later give us their opinions. We were secure in the support we had growing up and felt accepted and loved. If one of the older adults thought we were heading in the wrong direction, they would not hesitate to tell us. On Sundays, during the summer months, we would pile into Anthony's car as he drove Mary and us to Scarborough Beach for the day. Our friendships remained throughout our lives.

When we were in our late teens, and old enough to take the trolley or bus to Providence, we bought our clothing in more sophisticated stores. The three older children in our family were working. We handed our paychecks over to our father. I saved what our parents gave me, so I could buy clothes. Some of us worked more than one job.

Thursday nights were a big night in the city for my friends Elena and Beatrice Marino, Sylvia Palumbo, and me. It seemed the entire state of Rhode Island met in the streets of downtown Providence. It was always exciting to meet and socialize with friends. Having hot chocolate with our friends was the highlight of the week. We shopped at Shepherd's, Gladding's, Cherry and Webb, Peerless, the Outlet Store, Jeanne's, Sorority Shop, and upscale stores and boutiques. Often, we would tell our friends to meet us under Shepherd's clock, a well-known landmark. Shepard's Tea Room, a more sophisticated place, was a favorite place for lunch and tea. We met our friends in every coffee shop and diner that was popular.

When Garden City was developed, and we were in our twenties and married, we bought elegant knit suits at the Ida Leach Boutique.

Another favorite choice was going to Luke's, Chen's, or Ming Garden for Chinese food. Chen's located on Washington Street above City Hall Hardware was a favorite of me and my friend, Anna. Her mother would give each of us ten cents to buy chow mein, as well as ten cents for the bus fare to Providence. I took a bus to Anna's house often. If Uncle Alfred saw me waiting at the bus stop, he would stop his car and ask, "Where are you going, young lady?" He and his friend Victor Di Costa who was known as Have gun will travel or Paladin would take me to Anna's house.

We shared much over the years, especially the sewing club we had for over fifty years with our cousins. Joann, Anna, Lucy, Angela (Ialongo sisters), Mary Barone, Betty Paolella, Angie Cantone, and Irene Quintavallo (Cardi sisters) and I would meet at one of our homes regularly to sew, knit, or embroider. When we stopped with the projects, we still met for lunch at each other's homes. Mary would invite us to spend a day at her Scarborough Beach home during the summer months. We ate, played bocce, and recounted many family events. We would ask Irene what her secret was to longevity. She would pick up her small glass filled with red wine, and say, "A little with each meal is the answer, it's good for you."

When we were married and began to have children, most of them attended the same schools and became friends. Our relationships extend to the next generation, and we were thrilled. Going to a PTA meeting was joyful, as we socialized with our lifelong friends. Some of them became our neighbors.

Mama's cousin, Irene, brought her homemade baked goods, especially on holidays. The two women had much to talk about, and one could feel the joy and love they had for the other. Each year having a polenta party during the first snowstorm, was a ritual for the Domenico Cardi family. Mama was always included. Mary Barone would make the polenta, and each family would bring one of their specialty foods.

Cardi Cousins: Mary Barone, Elizabeth Paolella, Mama, Irene Quintevallo

Cousins Gaetanina and Angie Cardi Cantone Scarborough Beach

Cousins Angela Calvey and MarieVartanian

Cousins Bernadette and Joanne Healy

1ˢᵗ cousins: The Capotostos, Crudales, Miglioris.
Aunt Alene and Uncle Alfred's wedding

Marty's Spa and Cranston Social Club. Antonio B. Cardi Building

CHAPTER 15
THE WAY IT WAS

Christenings, First Communions, and confirmation were taken seriously. Our parents would empty one of the bedrooms, making it
into a dining room. The dinners would be catered by Frank George's,
Club 400, in later years called West Valley Inn. Frank George was the
popular caterer among the Italian community when planning large
events unless our mothers cooked the food themselves. When we were
kids, godparents were revered and honored. Our parents made sure their
children never forgot who they were. On holidays we had to visit our
godparents and bring them a gift. When we were preparing for our weddings, it was proper and expected that we hand-deliver an invitation to
our godparents, aunts, and uncles. Respect, it was called by our parents,
and it was mandatory.

I chuckle when I think of Aldo and Luke baking a cake for their godparents, Antonetta and Benny Soprano. While Mama and her girls were visiting the Soprano home one evening, Luke and Aldo entered the house, presenting a thinly layered cake on a platter. When Mama asked, "Why is the cake so thin?" they responded, "We forgot to add the baking powder." Mama was close friends with her commare, and her children, especially Virginia, Phyllis (Dodo), and Theresa. Joe Soprano (youngest son) later owned a grocery store. Frank (older son) and Virginia worked in the original Soprano's Market next door to Sinapi's Dry Good Store. Virginia was one of Mama's closest friends and confirmed me. We remained lifelong friends with the Sopranos.

During the summer months and early fall, several times a week, Mama walked to the vegetable stand of Santina Soprano on Phenix Avenue. Santina sold freshly picked garden vegetables from her garden. Many people bought their milk and corn from the local Del Bonis farm. When visiting Santina, Mama would often ask about her daughter, Sister Elisa, who was a close friend and confidante to Mama. We admired and respected Sister Elisa, and always listened attentively to her wisdom. Anna chose her name for confirmation. Theresa Soprano Miller, Anna Migliori Ferri, Frank Sinapi, Jr., and I were the same age, and we remained close friends. Our friends from Knightsville who settled in Oaklawn and our children carried on our close ties. Theresa settled in Connecticut. Ralph, our children, and I visited Theresa and Cliff Miller often at their home in Connecticut. We remained lifelong friends, and I baptized their daughter, Jennifer. Our neighbors Phyllis (Dodo) and Reggie Ricci were always there for Anna Izzo, and my family, as Ralph and I were for their family. We helped each other when one of us was in need. We were family to each other and had lifetime relationships. Dodo and Virginia baked like professionals. They were well-known for their gift of making fine pastries, gardening, and cooking many delicious meals. Many of Dodo and Virginia's recipes were written on small scraps of paper, which many of us still have in our possession.

Virginia Soprano Piotti

Bernadette, Frank Sinapi, Theresa Soprano Miller

Theresa Soprano Miller, Bernadette
Anna Migliori Ferri. Childhood friends and neighbors

Bernadette and Victor Palumbo

To the New Born King, He Pipes a Song

Benny Soprano playing La Zampogna (Providence Journal)

Benedetto [Bennie] Soprano played la zampogna (bagpipes) and was well-known for doing so, especially on Christmas Eve. According to an article in the Providence Journal, the "Zampognare" heralded Christmas with tunes played on the bagpipes by shepherds in Italy. Most of the Italian immigrants from Itri brought with them many traditions. They were true to all they knew and put into practice the skills they cultivated while living in Italy. Their beliefs and traditions were sacred to them.

The day after Easter, Easter Monday, Mama would place a large table, clothed with a white tablecloth, outside our door. She would display a variety of foods on the table. We would have a feast. Everything she made was delicious. Easter bread was a big expectation for the children. Making Easter bread was a long process. She made all of us individual bunnies, baskets, round rings made of Easter bread with eggs embedded in the dough, and loaves shaped as a cross. When she began to have grandchildren, she continued the tradition. The children couldn't wait to receive their bunnies. When the Itrani woman baked or cooked, it was for everyone, including family and friends. Parquet, or Pascone, as Mama called it, was a celebration. She would serve us all the foods she and her Nonna made on that day; torta di riso (rice pie), sweet bread, Pizza Rustica, pastiera Napoletana (ricotta pie) were Easter delicacies. At times we went to Skeleton Valley for a picnic, but mainly the celebration was in our yard (the small area in front of our apartment). We held sacred the traditions she taught us and practiced.

On Holy Saturday, Mama made the most delicious spinach pies, and we waited patiently to eat them. Mama was strict about fasting during Lent. We could not listen to the radio or watch television. To this day, I continue the practice of making spinach pies on that day.

Many friends and family would tease Mama, telling her to open a pizza parlor. For us, her pizza was the best. It always had that special flavor, just like all of her meals. We devoured her doughboys (pizza fritta) that were sprinkled with sugar. Most women made their dough. Making five pounds or more of fresh dough was not unusual. They would vigorously knead the dough made with King Arthur flour, place it in a large bowl, cover the bowl tightly and let it sit until the mixture rose and was ready to use. Kneading that much dough by hand was not easy. It required a lot of strength.

We may have been financially poor, but we were immensely blessed to have experienced such profound richness in our childhood.

To celebrate the feast of St. Joseph, Mama would make multiple trays of her famous, delicious, peasant zeppole sprinkled with sugar or honey for all of us - her children, brothers, sisters, and friends.

We couldn't wait for the Christmas Party the neighborhood children attended on the second floor of the Cardi building, above Marty's Variety Spa. Our uncles Alfred and Americo were members of the Cranston Social Club, and they made sure all of the children in Cardi's yard attended.

Christmas Eve, the feast of the seven fishes, is sacred to most Italian families. Our table was adorned with a festival of food. Fish and special family recipes were cooked with pride. Catholics abstain from eating meat on Christmas Eve. Seven represented the seven sacraments in our Catholic faith. We started our meals with a large antipasto platter made with pickled peppers we preserved in the fall, baccala, and snail salad. The light gravy was made with Mama's preserved tomatoes and tomato paste, (strata). The holiday, celebrating the birth of Jesus was taken seriously. Mama's culinary talents amazed me, as she ensured food choices for everyone. She made baccala, whiting or merluzzo, dressed in extra virgin olive oil, fresh lemon, and herbs (my favorite), for our first dish. Squid, smelts or calamari were other options. Spaghetti or linguini fini was served with shrimp or clams, and oglio olio was an option for those who did not like fish. Baked fish or baked stuffed shrimp were other alternatives. Vegetables were always a must, especially broccoli rabe. We ended all meals with a salad. Roasted chestnuts, Struffoli, fruit, pastries, and Jell-O with fruit for the younger children filled our table, as we cracked and ate nuts, the fruit, and dunked anise, and celery in a dish of olive oil mixed with black pepper and salt, at the end of our meal. Papa would play a game with us using hazelnuts. He would tell us that it was a game they played in Itri. It was fun.

Our Christmas tree went up on Christmas Eve before we had La Vigilia. There was much excitement wondering what we would get in our Christmas stockings, or if in fact, we would get anything. It was not unusual to get coal, a tangerine, and maybe a few nuts. That was a clear message that we had to behave if we expected Santa to give us what we want. Of course, we never did receive what we had dreamed of. We were poor, and simply happy to receive anything. Papa would go next door to the Sinapi store and buy something for each of us. Nothing was in abundance except food. We were grateful just to get a fresh tree. Recently, I heard that receiving a tangerine in our stocking represented receiving gold.

After Luke, my sisters, and I were married, we celebrated Christmas Eve together. It was fun for the children. In later years, each family celebrated with their own families. Usually, my husband Ralph or Victor Giannini, Maria Vartanian's husband, would dress as Santa Claus for the children, and our grandchildren. They were in awe as Santa talked with them and asked what they wanted for Christmas. There was much joy in our homes as we celebrated this holy, joyous feast together. Our children were always secure with their aunts and uncles and loved being with their cousins.

Our Thanksgiving wasn't much different from other holidays. Birthdays were special to us, and we celebrated them with great joy and love for one another. We never took our birthdays for granted. It was a special celebration for each of us in our family.

Another favorite celebration was the Fourth of July, at Aunt Mary and Uncle Bill Longo's home. All of the relatives were invited. The food was plentiful, and we had lots of fun. After taking the first bite of her delicious salad, I asked, "Aunt Mary what is the secret ingredient that makes your salad so tasty?" Smiling, she described, "I rub fresh garlic on the inside of the wooden salad bowl and mix it the regular Italian way." The regular Italian way meant mixed with our hands, with salt, extra virgin olive oil, and vinegar dressing, and whatever herbs one desired to add. Her salad had that special touch and flavor. Although she didn't tell me, I believe adding grandmother Maria Battista's homemade wine vinegar made the difference.

Jim Vartanian and Victor Giannini as Santa

Sr. Elisa Soprano

Conte coat of arms

CHAPTER 16
MEETING RALPH/MARRIAGE

I completed cosmetology school after I married Raffaele Gerardo (Ralph Charles) Conte, second son of Maria (Mary) Frances Conti, (daughter of Maria Martini and Raffaele Conti), and Paolo Conte (son of Maria Domenica and Ferdinando Conte) from Fondi, Italy, on a September 3, Labor Day holiday. Mary and Paolo had six children: Ferdinando (Fred), Raffaele (Ralph), Gloria, Paul, Richard, and William (twins). Ralph and I were married by our cousin Reverend Roland Cardi at St. Mary's Church. The reception was at DiLorenzo's 1025 Club, owned by a friend of Ralph's. In our era, we had double showers. Double showers were just as extravagant as weddings. Many of our showers took place at the Vilma Raye on Park Avenue. The goal was to give much financial support to the new couple. The full-course meals, which seemed costly at the time, were $2.50 to $3.25 per meal. Mama planned every bit of my shower and wedding. She chose the wedding cake made by Solitro's Bakery and what should be served for the meals. Pieces of fruitcake were inserted in white, satin boxes with our name and date printed on the cover, to give to the guests. Papa chose the favors (sets of rooster salt and pepper shakers), that he purchased from a wholesaler. I was the first to be married, and Papa was still living. They both wanted to be involved so that they would make sure everything was proper, non-fai scumbari. God forbid if they lost face.

Ralph's mother Mary, Mama, Zia Innocenza, made bushels of wandis sprinkled with confectioners' sugar, (small fried Italian cookies) in our kitchen. They were light and delicious. Ma Conte was known for her wandis. Trays of freshly baked cookies were made. The women were experts in making the Italian specialties. Everything had to be done according to Italian tradition, for my sisters and me.

After WWII, when Ralph returned home from the war, he studied photography at the Progressive School of Photography in Connecticut. I think about it at times, and realize that I was only 10 years old, and in the fourth grade at Knightsville School when the war ended, while Ralph was in the Philippines that day, on the USS PC 1123. I recall when our school principal, Miss Donnelly, announced to the class the war had ended. Most of us cried praying that times would get better, and our relatives and friends would come home quickly.

Ralph

Ralph, the photographer

Owner of Liberty Liquor Store

I was introduced to Ralph through his friend Stanley Shoemaker, who had come to live in Knightsville. Stanley opened a glass shop in our neighborhood, two buildings down from our house, in the former Soprano's Market. Each day as I left work, I would walk past his store to go to the mailbox with the day's mail. Stanley introduced himself and asked if I would mind meeting his wife, who felt alone in a new neighborhood. I feared Papa would find out that I had spoken with a stranger, let alone go to his house. I did not accept the invitation. After several weeks of Stanley's persistence, his wife asked me to visit her, and I agreed. Marie invited me to her apartment for coffee. While we were sitting at her kitchen table, we heard a knock at the door. She told the person to come in. It was Ralph, a handsome, well-dressed man. The four of us chatted while sipping coffee. Feeling shy and uneasy, I soon left for home. After that meeting, I seemed to encounter Ralph frequently, and we began to date. We were married two years later. When I married Ralph, he owned the Liberty Liquor Store in Providence. After the sale of the store in 1964, he remained in the wholesale liquor business.

Berndaette as teenager

Dating Ralph

Bernadette and Ralph

Going away party, Cardi's yard

Leaving for our honeymoon

In the pouring rain, the night before my wedding, Papa and his friend, Bambino Ruggieri, gave me the most beautiful serenade. Marie made me an elegant going-away suit, which she completed the night before the wedding. While the festivities were taking place, Marie was upstairs in our close friend Madeline Vellucci's second-floor apartment, sewing. I was in a state of panic, wondering if I would have a going-away outfit. As usual, Marie completed the Nile green, brocade dress, and matching coat at the eleventh hour.

Mama and Papa continued the wedding celebration by hosting a going-away party on the large open yard behind the drugstore, on the Cardi property (Cardi's yard, as we called it). Food and drink were abundant. We danced and sang to Papa's music. Mama planned everything to perfection. All of our friends and family members sent Ralph and me off with their blessings.

My first child, a son, was born a year later. I can still picture Mama and Papa coming to the Lying-In Hospital to see their first grandchild. Mama made sure her grandson was properly taken care of, with all of her natural methods. I was trying to implement all of what Dr. Spock said in his book, but Mama commanded, "Throw the book away, this is how you do it." And she made sure it was done her way. Thank God for the wisdom and knowledge of grandmothers.

I didn't have a chance after Mama held her first grandchild. She took right over. He became everyone's child. Often, Anna and Ronnie would spend the day with him. Marie spent a lot of time with him. He loved each of them and had a close bond with them. He called my sisters Mommy, that's how attached he was to them. Aldo, his godfather, gave him his first taste of macaroni when he was six months old.

Papa insisted I come to visit them daily. I walked from my Aldrich Avenue apartment, off Phenix Avenue, with the carriage or stroller if weather permitted. One spring day, I walked to their home, wearing capris and a cotton shirt. Papa took one look at me and reprimanded me for how I was dressed. He said, "You are a mother now, and you walked down Phenix Avenue dressed like that, aren't you ashamed?" I couldn't understand why he thought I was dressed improperly; I was fully covered. I guess he expected me to wear a dress. My sisters and I always had to look and dress properly and be ladylike. Papa loved fashion, and always dressed well.

When Mama became ill and needed surgery, Papa asked me to come to their house daily to cook for the family. He wanted to make sure Mama was taken care of, and that his single children had cooked meals.

Cousins: Ralph C. Conte Jr. and Rita Capotosto
Nonni and Papa's first two grandchildren

Christmas with Mama, Papa, Bernadette and baby Ralph

Papa holding his first grandchild Ralph C. Conte, Jr.

CHAPTER 17
UNEXPECTED CHANGES

At the age of 55, Papa became ill with pancreatic cancer. Mama never left his side caring for him around the clock. They didn't have a washing machine and dryer. Because of this, I shared every set of flannel and linen sheets Papa ever bought for me so that Mama would have enough for him.

Often, during his illness, he would insist on holding his first grandchild, Ralph Jr. Mama and I would prop him up on pillows and he would repeatedly say, as he held the baby, "How beautiful he is."

Aldo worked out of town and drove all night to get home. Papa waited for him before he passed. When Papa blessed Mama and all of his children with holy water before his death, we knew the blessing was a special gift for each of us. He had a holy and peaceful death. Weeping, we stood around his bed. He peacefully passed at the age of fifty-six with all of his family around him.

Later, after his death, Aldo took the business over, and it was renamed Columbia Imports. Aldo made a great personal and career sacrifice when he was asked by Papa minutes before his death, to take over the business for Mama.

We all felt the awful emptiness that accompanies the death of a loved one.

Mama never remarried. She was insulted when several men came to the house to ask for her hand in marriage. She was not amused by their advances. Angrily, she told them never to come back. During her illness before she passed, she said to my brother, Luke, "You find a nice woman and get married," and then pointed a finger at me and firmly said in Italian, "You're a widow now, don't ever be subject to anyone. Be free. Stay the way you are."

She worked hard to keep things together, with little money. Her faith got her through, with the help of those who were old enough to work, and still live at home. They supported the household. From our early childhood, many of us remembered when Mama would not even throw a parcel of bread away, without offering it up to Jesus, and for the souls in purgatory.

She derived much courage from her faith. She believed with all of her heart and soul that God would provide for her. She would tell us, "My faith and trust in God is my inheritance, and my six children are my money in the bank. She obtained strength from seeing and talking daily with Virginia and Antonetta Soprano while shopping at Soprano's Market and from her relationships with her cousins.

Raphael, Kali, Zoë, Ralph, Bernadette, Krishan, Katherine

CHAPTER 18
FAMILY GROWTH AND LOSS

Ralph and I built our home and moved to Oaklawn. Many of the kids we grew up with moved to the same area and became our neighbors. After living in a tenement house throughout their youth, they treasured having their own homes and took pride in caring for them.

Katherine Maria was our second child and was born five and a half years after the birth of Ralph, Jr. We felt blessed when our children were born. My sisters and I were pregnant at the same time. Katherine was the first girl to be born on January 16, Maria Vartanian Giannini January 26, and Deborah Izzo Ostrowski was born on February 23. Mama was thrilled that her girls had babies at the same time. Her first granddaughter Rita was six months younger than Ralph, and Dora was born in June, several months before the three girls. Mama loved children and had a special rapport with them. Being a female, she was not allowed to study medicine and to follow her dream of becoming a pediatrician. Having a special connection with children, they would do anything for her. Our sister Anna inherited that same quality.

Mama loved it when her daughters visited her often with their children of various ages. My sisters and I would scold Mama when she gave our children a cup of Hood's ice cream just before dinner. She would look at us and ignore everything we said. Turning to them she would say, "Good? Now, let's eat supper." Of course, we never expected our children to eat, but as usual with Mama, we were wrong. They ate everything. That was Mama. Don't defy her when it came to her grandchildren. Her greatest joy was when they were all together, playing at her home. When the girls were five or six-year-old, they freely went into her closet to fetch her high heels, put on one of her dresses and hats, and happily walked around showing off their grownup attire. Mama cherished every moment. They loved her and were spoiled by her. Her love was unconditional.

The families of my sisters and brothers did many things together. We spent many holidays together, celebrated each person's birthday, and loved and cared for each other. We were one family. All of our children loved their aunts, uncles, and cousins, and were secure with them. If one of the children needed discipline because they did something wrong, we would not hesitate to correct them. Cosmo and Aldo always imparted wisdom, direction, and love to our children.

Katherine and Ralph Conte

Ralph and Elisa Conte

Matthew and Katherine Melone

Matthew, Kali, Katherine, Krishan Melone, Ralph, Bernadette, Zoë, Elisa, Raphael Conte, Kelly Pisoli

Zoë Conte and Leo Matthew Murphy

Leo Matthrew Murphy, Jr.

Raphael Conte and Kelly Pisoli

Kali Rea Melone

Krishan M. Melone

Ralph and I were elated when our family began to expand. Ralph Jr. married Elisa Stufano, daughter of Carol Russo and Nicholas Stufano; they have a daughter Zoë, a son Raphael, and a grandson Leo Matthew Murphy Jr. Katherine married Matthew Joseph Melone, son of Rita Almeida and Edmond Melone; they have a daughter Kali Rea and a son Krishan Myo Ralph Jr. founded Raphael's Restaurant. He became highly acclaimed in the culinary world and spent 30-plus years in Providence. He studied and worked in the culinary field in various regions of Italy for several years. He and Elisa currently own Plum Point Bistro in Saunderstown. Elisa's (graphic artist and graduate of Rhode Island School of Design) artistic touch and design are evident in this restaurant as in all the previous restaurants. Their daughter, Zoë became involved with her parents and is the general manager. She works closely with her father. Raphael, Ralph, and Elisa's son also works as a manager at Plum Point Bistro.

Katherine lived in Rome for three years while studying at the Pontifical Gregorian. She is a graduate of North Eastern University and obtained graduate degrees from Providence College and Cal State, LA. Katherine works in mental health and lifestyle medicine. Currently, she is working toward licensure as a mental health counselor.

Katherine's husband Matthew is the founder of Focus Vision Media, a high concept media production company.

Gardening was Ralph's passion. Often, he was called upon to help neighbors, relatives, and friends with advice on how to choose and plant shrubs, prune trees, and design flower gardens. His yard was his pride and joy. He was possessive of his land and did not like my planting flowers in any old spot, as I sometimes did. I loved the wisteria arbor, his rose garden, the lilac and hydrangea bushes, and a variety of flowers he planted. He guided our daughter, Katherine, when she planted a garden of beautiful Irises. He was firm when it came to Ralph helping him maintain the yard. He made no bones about his son learning what he was taught by his father. His vegetable garden produced lots of fresh vegetables throughout the summer and fall. He and Dodo (our neighbor and lifelong friend) would spend hours discussing their favorite pastime, gardening. When someone complimented him about the yard, he would simply smile and say, "My father taught me well."

Ralph loved his work in the liquor industry. He was highly respected and trusted to always give the right advice. Countless times over the years, men would ask his advice about their business and especially if they were seeking to purchase a liquor store. Over the years, many young anxious men sat at my kitchen table while Ralph educated them about their jobs.

After serving the liquor industry for 50 years, Ralph passed on July 26, 2000, of a glioblastoma, multiforme stage 4. His faithful friends, Deborah and Howard Cliff, planned a celebration of his life at Raphael's

Bar-Risto in Providence, for the years of faithful service he gave to the liquor industry. Our son organized the event with twelve local restaurants who wanted to participate. His close friend Peter Aiello was supportive throughout Ralph's illness. Unfortunately, Ralph passed before the event. I was overwhelmed with emotion to witness the love, trust, and respect clients and friends throughout Rhode Island had for Ralph. He was a private person and never revealed to me, or anyone else information about the people he had helped. I was overcome with emotion when I heard the multitude of stories of how he had helped people over the years. It was obvious to me and my family that he was loved by many friends, family, and those in the liquor industry. His funeral was huge, and over six hundred people attended the celebration of his life.

Conte

The retirement party for

Ralph Conte

Monday, July 31, 2000

will continue as scheduled

"In Celebration of His Life"

Madonna della Civita Santuario

On the grounds of the Santuario, natives of Itri offering food and drink to me and friends

Enrico Cardi and Bernadette in Itri, Italy looking at historical documents

CHAPTER 19
MY FIRST TRIP TO ITALY

During the 1970s and 80s, I was heavily involved in the Charismatic Renewal and had an international ministry to leaders, priests, religious, and lay leaders. I was invited to attend the large international Charismatic Conference in Rome, Italy. It was being held at the Vatican and surrounding areas.

My children were young, and I didn't feel comfortable leaving them for ten days. Ralph said, "Bert, you may never have this opportunity again." Mama was ecstatic when I asked for her opinion and help with the children; she wanted me to meet her relatives and to visit Itri, her hometown.

I went to Italy with a group of close friends. Mama gave me the names and telephone numbers of Enrico, Cosmo and Carolina Cardi,

Zio Pasquale Cardi in Florence, Enrico's sister Vera who also lived in Florence, and Papa's brother Vincenzo who lived in Itri.

Nonno Onorato first prize winner for the best grapes and wine
Wine festival in Itri

Carol Cardi Trancoso, Dr. Alphonse Cardi's daughter, lived in Rome with her husband Alex, who was a medical student at the time. They were friendly with Tina and Enrico. I was welcomed with open arms by everyone, all because I was the daughter of Gaetanina Cardi.

Carol and Alex invited me to their apartment for dinner, along with Enrico and Tina. I felt an immediate connection with them. When I arrived at the apartment, I was greeted warmly. Tina presented me with a large bouquet of gladiolas. As we sat at the table, Enrico presented me with letters Mama had written to his mother Zia Loreta.

It was deeply touching. Carol and I wept when Enrico read the letters, which expressed the love and respect Mama had for Zia Loreto and her relatives. I felt blessed to have experienced this special moment with our cousins. Enrico explained the hardship Mama endured because of her aunt. He was emotional and angry. He told us of the hardship and trouble his father Zio Teodoro and his grandfather Zio Antonio went through to save Mama when her grandmother died. He told me in detail what had transpired to all involved, by the hands of this woman.

His bitterness was obvious when he told us of the circumstances and trials Zia Immocolatina had caused. The unhealed wounds were deep.

Enrico invited me to Itri, along with the priest who was on the trip with me and the group from Rhode Island. While attending the conference at the Vatican, we met people throughout the world, who gathered in Rome for the same purpose. Enrico invited a select few from our group to go to Itri with him. The priest and his friend accepted his invitation. Enrico insisted that the priest sleep in his home in Itri. I was told I had to stay with my Capotosto relatives.

When Enrico stopped the car in Itri, he pointed and said, "Look." Sitting on a chair in the piazza talking with other men, was Zio Vincenzo Capotosto, Papa's brother. It reminded me of the men who would stand in front of Marty's Spa in Knightsville when we were young. I could feel my heart beating. Zio Vincenzo looked so much like Papa.

I went up to him and told him I was his niece. He greeted me and took me to his daughter's home. It was like having a little piece of Papa once again. I met his daughter Ilda (Hilda) and her husband Salvatore, Nicolina, the daughter from his wife's first marriage, and his son Sergio.

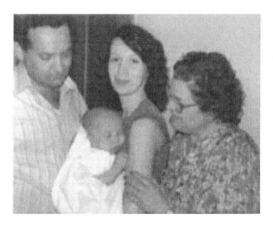

Dr. Alex and Carol Cardi Troncoso holding baby Alex and Tina Cardi. Dinner at the Conte home

Zio Vincenzo Capotosto

Ilda, Bernadette, Vincenzo, and Amalia Capotosto, Ilda's son

They were kind and cordial to me. Hilda invited me to her home for a fabulous dinner, with many of the Capotosto relatives who lived in Itri. I was told that their brother Dante had died of encephalitis at a young age.

I asked Enrico why I had to stay at my uncle's home. He emphatically said, "That is your father's family. It's proper for you to stay with his family.

Enrico took me into his house in Itri and showed me where Mama and Amedeo (Father Roland Cardi) slept, and one of the stoves that I had heard so much about. He took me and my friends to the Santuario di Maria SS. della Civita, where the American priest Reverend Lionel Blaine served Mass.

Father Blaine spoke Italian, and introduced me to the natives of Itri, explaining who I, my parents, and ancestors were. Happily, they said they knew Mama and Papa. As they turned to greet me, many exclaimed, "Ah, figlia di Gaetanina e Cosmo." They also knew all of the Cardis and Capotostos who lived in Itri. I felt as if I was experiencing the Visitation, when Mary went to the hill country for three months, to stay with her cousin Elizabeth. I can still visualize the colorful kerchiefs on the heads of the native women, while they were in church.

When the Mass was over, on the sanctuary grounds, all kinds of food and drink were set up on the outside picnic tables by natives of Itri (This practice is no longer allowed). We were invited to eat. It was one of the most thrilling parts of my trip, going to Itri, experiencing the warmth, and being welcomed by people who knew Mama and Papa, our ancestors, and feeling the admiration, respect, and love they had for them.

Fr. Lionel Blaine celebrating Mass at the Santuario

Sergio, serving Katherine and me figs from Nonno Onorato's land, Itri

Enrico getting historical documents for Bernadette

Zio Cav. Pasquale Cardi with Bernadette Florence, Italy

On the way back to Rome from Itri, Enrico showed me and my friends Gaeta and the surrounding beautiful beach towns of Sperlonga and Terracina.

I felt bad for Fr. Blaine. He was the only person in our group who spoke fluent Italian. He became somewhat tired of making phone calls for me to relatives in Italy, to explain I was figlia di Gaetanina Cardi from America.

One of these times was when he called Cavalier Zio Pasquale Cardi, who lived in Florence. Mama wanted me to meet Zio Pasquale, whom she loved and corresponded with. He immediately came to the pensione we were all staying at, to check on the people I was with. After meeting my friends, he told Father Blaine and me that it was okay for me to stay there, and to be with the group. Members of our group were amazed that Zio Pasquale, a dignified man, emphatically told me he approved of the people I was traveling with. It was clear to us that he was watching out for his niece's daughter.

He instructed me to be ready the following morning to go out with him. He took a bus to the pensione, and we, in turn, took a bus to his home. When we arrived at his home, he showed me his art collection, displayed on every space, and on every wall in his home. He told me he collected art and antiques and went out each day to antique shops. I was deeply impressed. When I went home, I began placing pictures that had meaning for me along my hallway wall, and throughout my home. I loved him immediately. Zio Pasquale had the utmost respect and love for Mama. He was a man of class and dignity. The more time I spent with Mama's relatives, the more I loved them and wanted to know more about them.

While I was at Zio Pasquale's house, he called Enrico's sister Vera who lives in Florence, to tell her I was there visiting. She invited us to her home. I was impressed with her beautiful home, especially with the middle floor. It was a cantina, a place where they stored wine, large vats of olives, cheese, olive oil, and other delicious edibles. Her husband explained to me the front entrance doors of their home were replicas of the Vatican doors.

The culture, food, and art were exceptional. I loved every moment and experience. I was proud of our heritage, and the love our relatives still had for Mama. I was treated with the utmost respect and love because I was her daughter. I was welcomed with open arms just by the mere mention of her name. I believe Mama wanted me to experience a taste of how she grew up, with people she loved and who loved her. I understood more thoroughly the loneliness she must have felt for what she left behind.

My group stayed at convents in Rome, not far from the North American College. Daily Enrico would meet me and my friends. After socializing, he would take me to his home. As usual, Tina would cook a fantastic meal. It was at one of these daily social meetings with my group, that Enrico invited the priest and others to Itri.

Father Rick (not the correct name), a native of Cranston, Rhode Island, was also a priest at the time and a professor, teaching at the North American College. He came to meet me at the convent, and showed me around the Jewish section of Rome, pointing out many historical buildings where Popes had lived. I was enlightened with much history. Rick knew Mama and took me to a jewelry store to buy earrings for her. He chose the earrings, and I purchased them. I was grateful to him for taking me to a store he knew sold 18-carat gold. Mama loved them, especially when I told her Father Rick had chosen them.

I was fascinated by the culture and history in Rome. Each section I went to was interesting and full of history that I knew little of. Our group was blessed to have Father Blaine travel with us. Having lived in Rome himself, he knew areas and history that we would not have seen or known about. He was our personal tour guide.

Years later, couples and friends who went on the same trip talked about how blessed we were to be with people from around the world, worshipping and singing praises to Our Lord.

Even as we rode the buses each day, we heard songs in all languages, but one would never know it. Groups from various countries gathered with us at the catacombs as we sang in different languages and celebrated our lives in the spirit. We were one in Christ. It was a one of a kind, unforgettable experience. Pope Paul VI celebrated Mass for us at Saint Peter's and gave us his apostolic blessing.

A group of us, priests, nuns, and the laity later went to Lourdes for an overnight. I never experienced a more wonderful, spiritual place in the entire world. People throughout the world, who spoke in all languages, came to pray to Our Lady of Lourdes. Thousands of people were there in wheelchairs or were on stretchers seeking a miracle. The Lourdes waters are claimed to be healing. People drink it, put it on their bodies, or go into the baths, as I did. I was speechless when I came out of the baths and was dry. Lourdes is one of my favorite places in the entire world. It is the place to go to when one is desperately ill without medical hope, or if one is troubled. People simply go there to experience the powers of faith. One never leaves Lourdes empty-handed, or without some sort of conversion and blessing. Mainly, people go to honor our heavenly mother. As her children, we go to our mother when we are in trouble, always asking for her help.

Grotto of Our Lady of Lourdes, France

Enrico pouring wine forRalph at the Cardi home in Itri

CHAPTER 20
ENRICO BRIDGING THE GAP
BETWEEN THE NEW AND THE OLD

It seemed as if anyone who went to Italy was told to telephone Enrico and his wife Tina. They did not have any children but had a large extended family.

Weekly, they went to Itri for the weekend. When Enrico took my friends and me to Itri, he showed us many interesting and historical sites, including the Santuario.

He was proud of his olive trees, wine cellar, and albums of family photos and historical documents. The wine bottles had dust and webs on them, but he refused to dust them off. He wanted everything to remain natural and old-looking. He would stand at the table and pour wine from one of the canteens. He was proud of all he did to preserve history, and to show his relatives from America that the old was the best. Before I left for America, Enrico gave me an olive branch to give to Mama. He said, "She left Itri after much turmoil and trials. I want you to bring her a symbol of peace from Itri and me."

He took me to the Capuchin Monastery, the church of Santa Maria Maggiore, and showed me the Chiesa di San Michele. He pointed out the place where Mama had lived. I went to see Cosmo Cardi in the Esso station (now ENT) in the heart of Itri. Cosmo immediately took me to the home of his sister, and Mama's cousin and best friend Carolina. I was greeted with open arms, for the two women loved each other. I did not meet Titolinda, Carolina's sister. He took me to the places Mama wanted me to see. Gianpaolo Cardi and his nephew, Valerio, now own the gas station.

The second time I returned to Italy was when my daughter, Katherine, decided to study at the Pontifical Gregorian in Rome. Again, Enrico took us to Itri, and we stayed with the widow of Zio Vincenzo and her son Sergio. Sergio took us figs he picked from what was once Nonno Onorato's land. Although Papa and Angelina inherited their portion of the land, it was given to Vincenzo for his family. Papa regularly sent money to his father to pay for this land. He and our family sacrificed much and did without so that Papa could help his family in Itri. This land was also where Nonno Onorato grew the best grapes in Itri. He won many prizes for having the best grapes and wine during Itri's yearly wine festival. I was sad to hear on my last trip to Itri in 2013, that the land is now sold because of poor judgments that Sergio made.

I remember Papa mailing packages with all kinds of necessities, even toilet paper, and many other goods to help with their daily survival. I also remember clearly when he bought and sent a wedding dress to his niece, Nicolina.

To teach me about his family and how to write in Italian, he would ask me to write letters to Nicolina, which he dictated. I didn't know how to write in Italian. When I questioned Papa he would say, "Write the word as I pronounce it. Try, that's how you will learn.

Katherine walked throughout Itri taking photos. We spent a lot of time with Enrico and Tina. Tina was a fabulous cook and we had dinner with them most of the time. We cherished the days we spent at the beach, Vendicio. Later we would purchase fresh baby clams in a local fishing town, and Tina would make delicious spaghetti alle vongole. The buffalo mozzarella was freshly made and was the best I had ever eaten.

Katherine and I looked in amazement at the Montagna Spaccata (Split Mountain) in Gaeta. Tina and Enrico explained the history of the places they took us to. I was grateful to Tina and Enrico, for first-hand information and knowledge regarding each place they took us to.

According to the legend, at the time when the Saracens were overrunning Europe, a Turkish pirate, who did not believe that the rock had split at the death of Jesus, touched the rock and said, "If this is true, then let this rock become liquid." As he spoke, the rock liquified and gave way to the imprint of his hand. You can put your fingers into the handprint today! (Catholicism Pure and Simple).

Tina Cardi and Katherine Conte Montagna Spaccata

Ralph taking photos at the site of the imprinted hand. Sanctuary of the Holy Spirit Montagna Spaccata (Split Mountain) Gaeta, Italy

When Katherine lived in Rome for three years, Ralph and I visited her. It was Ralph's first trip, and Katherine took us on a grand tour of southern Italy including Itri. We stayed at the Hotel Sarapo, the Capotostos own in Gaeta above the Montagna Spaccata (Split Mountain). It was a glorious spot, and the beach below the hotel was beautiful.

We visited Fondi, the town that Ralph's parents and ancestors came from. We went into a travel agency that was named Capotosto. I asked if we were relatives. The man responded that he originally came from Itri, and we were probably related.

As we were talking, he motioned to a young man who was visiting him. He told us his name. I asked if he was related to Paolo Di Biase. He replied, "Paolo is my grandfather." I was excited when I heard it, and responded, "Paolo is our cousin." Mr. Capotosto told us to wait with him and sent the young man to tell his grandfather that relatives were there from America.

Quickly, Paolo entered the office, and when he heard I was the daughter of Gaetanina, he began to cry. He insisted that we go to his home. This meeting was an unexpected surprise.

Immediately, Zia Filomena began making home-made pasta. We had a fabulous dinner with them, along with his son Alfonso, his wife Giana, and their children. It was a memorable part of our trip. When Zio Paolo talked about Mama, tears rolled down his cheeks, as he told us how sorry he was that his mother had caused her so much trouble. They are a wonderful family, and Katherine visited them at times when she lived in Rome.

Zio Paolo Di Biase greeting Katherine, Ralph and me Fondi, Italy)

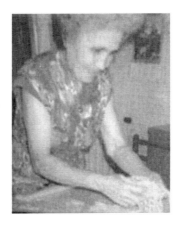

Zia Filomena Di Biase making homemade pasta,

Uncle Rico invited Tina and Enrico to visit Cranston. It was their first trip to America. He and Aunt Jeanette took Tina and Enrico to many places and entertained our relatives at their home. Many of us brought pastries, pizza, and other foods to share with our relatives. Vera Cardi, Alphonso's wife would take her preserved cracked green olives. We shared the responsibilities that were needed, to entertain relatives and friends.

Tina and Enrico stayed at the home of Aunt Maria Civitina Longo (Mary) when they returned to America the second time. She entertained numerous relatives who came to visit the couple. Some of us helped with the food, entertainment, and travel. Ralph and I took Tina, Mama, Aunt Mary, and Aunt Alene to Maine one of the times.

I hosted an anniversary party in my backyard for Tina and Enrico. Many relatives and friends attended. We sang to live music, and it was a joy to see the love and respect our families had for one another.

When each relative from Italy came to America, my home was the hospitality center for all of the relatives. I would cook a large dinner and invite member of my family, aunts, uncles, and cousins from Antonio, Domenico, and Vincenzo Cardi families to visit with our guests. It was exciting for me. Mama would usually say, "Betta, my house isn't big enough, you do it for me." I loved every moment and felt in tune with my heritage from Itri, Italy. I felt the connection, especially the one they had with Mama because she grew up with them. They were still family, and they had a deep, mutual love and respect for one another.

Tina singing a with musician

Anniversary party for Tina and Enrico at the Conte home

Bernadette and Enrico dancing

Each of Mama's cousins - Enrico and Tina Cardi from Roma and Itri, Paolo Di Biase from Fondi, Dr. Antonio Cardi from Caserta, and Zio Vincenzo Capotosto visited my home. They were interesting, educated, and displayed strong emotions towards Mama and other relatives they had the opportunity to meet at my home. The Domenico Cardi family also had a reception with many of our relatives for cousins Professor Mario and Dr. Ettore Cardi from Itri and Rome. I recall one of our relatives and his wife visiting Dr. Antonio Cardi in Caserta. Not knowing who they were, Antonio wasn't cordial or welcoming to the couple. Discouraged, before the couple was about to leave, the gentleman mentioned Mama and said they were a close relative of hers. It was then that Antonio greeted them warmly and entertained them for the evening.

The first time I went to Italy, I was greeted with open arms, and with much love and respect, all because of the love and respect they had for Mama. I fulfilled everything she told me to do and to bring her love to her relatives with whom she had a close, strong bond. I feel blessed that I had this opportunity in my life, and that she opened the door for me and my children to know and experience the relationships we developed with our relatives from Italy.

CHAPTER 21
GAETANINA'S RETURN TO ITRI

Katy is what Mama was called by family and friends when she came to America. I was told repeatedly by many relatives that Mama was beautiful, well-dressed, and classy when she lived in Itri. She maintained the classiness when she lived in America.

In 1977, Mama needed a passport in preparation for her trip to Italy. I wanted to know what her baptismal name was, for she was called Gaetanina, Gaetana, Caterina, Catherine, and Katy. Mama was consumed with fear when I told her I would apply for a passport for her. I reassured her that everything would be proper. With terror, she cried, "No, no, I will be arrested. Zia Immocolatina will hurt me."

I had never seen Mama so frightened. I replied, "Ma, this is a different period in time and a different country. You have a family to protect you now. It will be all right, I promise.

Little did I know what to expect when searching for her records. It seemed that Mama did not exist. When I went to the Cranston City Hall, the clerk could not find any record of her birth. Aunt Alene Cardi accompanied me, while I unsuccessfully searched records at the original St. Bartholomew's Church in Cranston. Searching further, we went to St. Rocco's Church in Johnston (Thornton), Rhode Island. The pastor at St. Rocco's Church could not find any Gaetanina Cardi or Caterina Cardi. Discouraged and desperate to fulfill my promise to Mama, I asked him if I could go through the book to look for a familiar name or clue.

He agreed. As I looked at each name, I noticed the names of Antonio Conde/Conte and Maria C. Saccoccio. Mama's name was listed as Gaetana Conte. I went back to the City Hall to again search for records of her birth. The clerk could not find any records of her. I began to panic, as I returned to St. Rocco's Church to ask the pastor for a copy of Mama's baptismal certificate. Expressing my concern for the recorded errors of her name, the priest made notes in the margin of the page, correcting the last name to Cardi. Named for her paternal grandmother Gaetana, Mama was referred to as Gaetanina, "Little Gaetana," throughout her life.

Determined and desperate to find her records, I returned to the Cranston City Hall with the corrected copy of her birth certificate. Records were finally found, indicating that Mama's birth was registered on April 12, 1923, by Dr. Angelo G. Fidanza, even though she was born on June 17, 1908. On February 20, 1924, her father Antonio Cardi, legally changed her name to Caterina. Throughout Itri, she was known as Gaetanina. I never heard her friends and relatives call her Caterina. The explanation given to Mama was that her sister, Anna, did not like the name and wanted her to be called Caterina. To please his daughter Anna, Antonio changed Mama's name. Little did they know what this change would cost Gaetanina.

After investigating and researching her birth records, I was left with many perplexing questions that will never be answered. Years back, a language barrier between the Americans and immigrants existed, as it does today. It was easy, and common for names to be recorded incorrectly, as it was on her baptismal records. I noticed on some of the census records, that Aunt Anna's name was often listed as Nina. Mama's name was misspelled and listed incorrectly many times. I couldn't help but wonder why Antonio would deliberately change the name of his daughter, Gaetana. The child was given her grandmother's name at birth. It didn't make sense to me that he would give his child a different name, especially after his mother had cared for and raised her. Dishonoring his mother in this way, didn't fit the description of the Antonio I heard so much about. His beliefs and family honor were major factors in his life.

I found it strange that his daughter's birth was not registered soon after her birth. Why did he change her name legally, after many years had passed? Did all of this confusion happen when a new passport application was filed, for her return trip to America, or when her father applied for a passport when he took her to Italy? Did the person filling out the documents, and recording them for Antonio, make the errors? It's possible when Antonio pronounced her name as Gaetanina, or Gaetana, the clerk could have easily misinterpreted her name as Caterina. The explanation given is questionable. It seemed there was great confusion surrounding Mama's name, life, and destiny. I felt sad for her and the fears she carried with her throughout her life, because of what her aunt had done to her, and for being sent to another country far away from the family she knew.

It has always been unclear why her father did not return to Itri to take his daughter home after he remarried. Did Gaetana and Alfonso insist she stay with them? I've heard it said that Antonio wanted his daughter to stay in Itri, to help his mother. I don't know if this statement is true. Whatever the reason, this decision left lifelong deep wounds and emotional rejection in Gaetanina. She never understood and carried a deep hurt and rejection within her, not understanding why her father chose to keep her in Itri, away from her family, and why he seemingly was indifferent to her.

After I made sure all of her legal papers were correct, and she received a passport, I was able to breathe a sigh of relief. I never revealed to her what I discovered and how uneasy I felt trying to obtain the proper documents.

Ralph and I hosted a going-away party for Mama in our backyard. Many friends and relatives attended, wishing her a safe and happy trip. The family and her close friends were ecstatic for her.

I bought her a new wardrobe so that she would travel light (so I thought), and gifts for her relatives and friends.

The following day, our family took her to the airport. I remember standing with my brothers and sisters, their spouses, and our children waiting for the departure of her plane from Logan Airport in Boston.

Mama said her goodbyes to all of her family, and I was suddenly unsure about her leaving. My only comfort was that she would be flying on the same plane with a close family friend, Carmella. Carmella reassured us that she would watch over Mama. Overcome with fear, I said to Ralph, "If anything happens to her, I will never forgive myself for insisting she go to Italy. Didn't I continually reassure her it would be safe?" The only consolation I felt was that her cousin Enrico Cardi, who lived in Rome, would pick her up at the airport and take her to Itri, 91.6 miles away.

When we returned home, I tried to stay focused on the wonderful going-away party I gave for her at my home. Her send-off by relatives and friends was filled with love and good wishes.

Several days after her arrival in Itri, she phoned me and family members. She excitedly proclaimed, "Betta, thank you, I love it, I'm home. I want to stay. I'm with my cousins, Carolina and Titolinda. I don't want to come home." I couldn't believe what I was hearing. She was extremely happy and excited being in her homeland, fulfilling her longing to be with her people. She cried out, repeatedly, "Betta, I'm home." Her relatives loved and accepted her unconditionally. Carolina and her sister, Titolinda, were her closest childhood friends and cousins. Their brother, Cosmo Cardi owned the Esso gas station (now ENT) in Itri. Their house was located on the street behind the gas station, on the backside of the building where Zio Teodoro Cardi lived. That is where she stayed when she returned to Italy. My anxiety and fears seemed to melt away when I heard the excitement in her voice.

Before coming home, she gave all of her clothes away to friends and family. Giving without reserve, that was who she was.

Baptismal Certificate and Corrected baptismal certificate
St. Rocco's Church

Dr. Luigi, Gianpaolo, Cosmo, Gaetanina, Carolina, Titolinda Cardi

*ENT gas station that Gianpaolo Cardi owns with his nephew Valerio
Carolina's house, is in the building behind the gas station*

Una notte del 1943
nella campagna di Itri

Avventura drammatica con due soldati tedeschi

a cura di Ettore Cardi

CHAPTER 22
A NIGHT IN THE COUNTRYSIDE OF ITRI IN 1943 (ETTORE CARDI)

I visited Italy again in 2013. I went to Rome with my nieces Dora, Rita, Jacqueline, and Jacqueline's husband Sam. I met with my friend Rosalba Martini Belfiori while the others toured Rome. Rosalba and I had dinner at Ettore Cardi's home. He reviewed events and the different branches in our family history with me. Tina was at Ettore's home, and we reminisced about her visits to Rhode Island.

Ettore presented me with a copy of his book, *A Night in the Country-side of Itri, 1943*. It is a documented story of a dramatic adventure with two German soldiers and a remarkable story that brings awareness to those of us who have not experienced the ravages of war.

When Ettore handed me his book he said, "Do whatever you want with it." I had the book translated into English and decided to add the account of the story in this book for all to read. My intention in doing so is that the younger generations will know what our relatives and ancestors endured for freedom, especially from dictatorship and communism. I revere and applaud their courage, faith, and strength in protecting their families, faith, and lives.

A Night in the Countryside of Itri, 1943

Introduction

The present publication is owed to the kind request of Dr. Marisa de'Spagnolis, archaeologist, and a passionate enthusiast of all things having to do with Itri, to whom, not long ago, I recounted the facts of what had occurred and here recounted. It also seemed to be opportune to disclose this.

The episode, which happened in Itri during the Second World War, is rare and perhaps unique, in this period in our country. It deals with the disarmament of two German soldiers, who with a pistol in hand, presented themselves at night at our country house looking for signorine. The two soldiers were disarmed by my father and brothers, who were unarmed civilians. This is how it happened on November 12, 1943, in the countryside of Itri, where the population of the area had gone, almost totally, due to the advancement of the front, set up on the Garigliano. The area where these events took place is called "Monticelle" and is located behind the cemetery of Itri.

I can only add a few things in respect to what my brother Mario recounted, in a statement deposited in the Archivio di Stato di Latina on June 10, 1996, that is published in this book. I remember on that night I was sleeping on the first floor, where the women of the family were, because I was the youngest of the brothers, being 14 years old. Near midnight, we heard a loud sound of voices coming from the stairs that led to the first floor, where we were. When I looked, I saw a group of men illuminated by the light of a few candles, in the small space near the landing and first stairs, which were about ten feet away from where we were. In the space, there were two German soldiers, held immobilized by my brother and my father, who was speaking to them indignantly. One of them, in order to ask for benevolence, said, "I, Tarvisio," in order to communicate that he was from Tarvisio, a small Italian village at the border of Austria. My father said, "Okay, you Tarvisio," and gave him another slap.

In juxtaposition to the miserable image of these two soldiers, almost as a life lesson to never generalize, emerges from the story of my brother Mario the wonderful figure of another German soldier, apparently belonging to the same unit, that was an anti-aircraft battalion that was based within a couple of days of the cemetery of Itri. He was a secular brother of the Franciscan convent of Grottaferrata (Rome), summoned to arms as a soldier in the Flak (German anti-aircraft battalion). His religious name was fra Antimo, but as a soldier, he went by Giorgio, his original name. Giorgio was chosen to be the interpreter in a trial by a military tribunal that quickly became well-known for the two German soldiers, paradoxically not for the crime that they had committed, but because they allowed themselves to be disarmed by Italian civilians. Giorgio became a very dear friend of the family, and he came to find us numerous times –during those sad days after the war when he found himself in the Franciscan convent of Grottaferrata, then in that of Castel Sant'Elia (Viterbo), and then in the German convents of Bad Tolz and Dettelbach a Main.

At this point, I need to include that which is reported by my brother Mario, with a memory of a relevant episode concerning Giorgio. There was a certain moment that passed a couple of days after the night of the disarming, in which the German commander of the battalion planned a nocturnal visit on behalf of the military to our country house. This visit, above all because it was happening at night, did not mean anything good: he could easily deport the men who had disarmed the soldiers. Here, Giorgio secretly informed the family of the visit, with extreme personal risk, for if he had been caught, there would certainly have been very serious repercussions.

I remember, to give an idea of the atmosphere of the time, that there was a family meeting to decide what to do. At the meeting, there was a Sicilian soldier who lived with us, because he was not able to reach his home, that was Troina (Enna) in Sicily, because of the front along the Garigliano River. Antonio Trovato (that was the soldier's name) proposed that we transform the house into a little fortress. He suggested that we close all of the entrances, cut down an orange tree that grew in the back of the house, and which they could have climbed and entered the house, and that we defend ourselves with hand grenades that he possessed. *This plan was not followed because it did not seem realistic. We adopted another idea, as you will see.*

It was decided that during the night that Giorgio had indicated, the men who had participated in the disarming of the soldiers would have to get away from the house in order to be cautious. The remaining family members, as advised by Giorgio, only appeared to sleep, because they were waiting for the visit from the Germans. Right on time, during the night, we heard an intense sound, and a little while later, a knock on the door and they came into the house. The house was surrounded by other military officers, along with an official of the battalion who was accompanied by Giorgio, of whom I still remember his long gun. The official invited us, with courtesy, to vacate the area, the reason in the days that followed that the family separated: the sisters Sofia, Wanda, Vera, and my mother Loreta Di Mascolo went to Roma, my older brother Mario and I went to Cessena, now the province of Forli, where he taught at the Istituto Tecnico Agrarian, now "Arnaldo Mussolini." My brothers Enrico and Giuseppe, and our father Teodoro, were forced to work for the anti-aircraft battalion, to whom the official belonged. He had planned the nocturnal visit that was described above. After they found refuge in the mountains of Itri, in the area of Raelle, when the unit was transferred far from Itri, the same official procured for members of the family the necessary permits to be able to travel to Priverno, where the train could be taken to and from Rome. One of these passes, the one issued to me, is published.

I would also like to relate two memories of my father, relative to that night, based on the recent suggestion of my sister Vera, while I was preparing this publication. Giorgio told us that one of the disarmed soldiers said, alluding to my father: "The old one had the strength of a lion." The second of the two memories concern the words that he had said to my brothers during the conflict: "Show that you are men."

Ettore Cardi
Rome, March 20, 2008

Document 1. Copy of a statement given to the Archivio di Stato di Latina by Mario Cardi, June 10, 1996, where the facts of November 12, 1943, are recounted.

With the intent to guarantee the conservation of a personal testimony relative to an episode that occurred during the Second World War, I give to the Archivio di Stato di Latina the original of a document left January 17, 1974, at Bad Tolz (Germany) by the notary WILHELM, BENGL.

The episode about which is testified by the monk of Grottaferrata NEUBAUER, GIORG already interpreter for the 4th anti-craft battalion of the German military stationed in Itri, and which involved the family of the writer Professor Cardi, Mario and appears in the following testimony. I am also including a photocopy of the document with a photo of the quoted monk during his military service in the German military.
Latina, June 10, 1996

In faith,
Mario Cardi

Prof. Mario Cardi
Born in Itri (LT) 5/15/1912
Resident of Latina
Via dello Statuo,

Explanatory memory of the episode
　　It was November 12, 1943, the German troops had militarily occupied the entire zone, where the Italian military, without command and without direction, was liquefied like dust in the wind.

　　At the time, our family was made up of Teodoro and Loreta, our parents, their children Mario, Sofia (27 years old), Wanda (23), Vera (22), Enrico and Peppino (almost 20), Ettore, and our maternal grandfather Antonio Di Mascolo. About 15 days prior, in order to evade the bombings and abuses of the badly intentioned military, all of the family, like almost all of the inhabitants of the area, had left the city of Itri, and had transferred themselves to one of our properties, located in the region of Monticelle, a hilly area encircled by mountains, still in the area of Itri.

　　Near the 9th or 10th of November, in the same zone, right near the cemetery of Itri, a German anti-aircraft battalion set up camp with a large number of soldiers. In the afternoon of the 12th, two soldiers arrived at the house in search of eggs; they made themselves known to the people and were granted their request. Everything seemed to be fine, and after an outdoor supper eaten by candlelight, the family went to rest in a pre-arranged manner: my father Teodoro in one room, also used as a stable, two brothers in another room that was used to store wood, the writer Mario in a narrow landing on the first floor, and all of the rest of the family in a single room on the first floor.

But near midnight, the same soldiers who had come searching for eggs appeared armed with pistols and daggers, and this time they were not searching for eggs, but instead, women. The first to wake up was my father, to whom they asked for a "flame," that is light, and asked, "Where are the women?" My father pretended to be a passerby, and a beggar who knew nothing. They moved on to the room with the brothers, who were forced, under the threat of violence, to pull out the bed, mattresses, and the poor-quality goods.

The only thing that remained was to go to the first floor, where the women were, and under the threat of violence, forced my father to call me to open the door from the inside. I opened the door and I found myself face to face with a pistol and a dagger pointed at my chest. Everyone together started to climb the stairway, illuminated by a faint oil lamp on the wall. When the soldiers were on the landing, separated only by a fragile door from the room where my grandfather, mother, and sisters were, my father without warning, in a decisive and unconditional way said, "Go ahead! Let's get them!"

And here begins the drama: my father, pinning his arms from behind, immobilized the German, blocking him from using his pistol. In the meantime, the light fell, and we remained completely in the dark; my father ordered me to take the pistol, which more than once touched me below the chin.

The first one remained disarmed, the second in a struggle with my brothers, Enrico and Peppino, at the top of the stairs; I heard a moan like that of someone who was gravely injured. I asked, "Enrico, where is the German?" "He is here," he responded. At the beginning of the conflict, in fact, with the help of Peppino, he had gotten to his neck and had immediately wrapped his hands around it, strangling him.

I then asked, "Light, light," in a loud voice, my poor mother only then opening the door, lighted three or four lights.

When the aggressors realized that they were at our mercy, completely and absolutely, they began to pray, begging us not to kill them and asking for forgiveness. In truth, my father, the parent who was most hurt by their attempt, because he had seen the possibility of the loss of honor for his daughters, was not feeling very generous or magnanimous toward two rascals and gave Enrico the pistol and told him to kill them. Our imploring Enrico caused him to reconsider, and he did not resort to extreme measures.

Therefore, already disarmed, they were searched and deprived of personal documents and items.

Around 3:00 am, the night still upon us, after a furious conflict that fortunately did not turn into a tragedy, almost as if they had won the day, the two were let go and perhaps it was an act of excessive generosity because they could have returned with others and better armed to retaliate, which fortunately did not happen.

Being left alone, we realized that it was not a good idea to remain at the house, due to the fear of a return of the soldiers for an act of retaliation. The women, my grandfather, and the youngest of the brothers found generous hospitality amongst the neighbors. My brothers and I decided to escape to the mountains and we wanted to bring our father Teodoro with us, the instigator and the cause of the resistance, but he who had the courage of a lion wanted to remain alone for the rest of the night, to defend his house.

After the episode, on the road of the mountain, I had a particular state of mind in which I was prepared to become an outlaw, a partisan, also a bandit spurred by the events of the night.

It is necessary to recount a marginal episode that demonstrates the generosity and courage of my brother Enrico: at the base of the mountain, we remembered that as a guest of our family, there was a Sicilian soldier, named Antonio Trovato who, after the 8th of September, was not able to reach his family in Sicily because of the front beyond the Garigliano, and who slept in a tent with a haversack and a hand grenade; for this reason, he ran the risk of being discovered and killed. My brother Enrico made us stop; he returned back to the house, passing with great risk near the German camp, woke him up and brought him with us into the mountains.

In the meantime, the dawn appeared that found us reunited in a little woodcutter's hut in the high part of Montemarano, which was habitually used as a refuge to flee from the Germans' search.

After the conflict:

In the afternoon of that day, I looked out into the valley and I saw all that would normally be. There was smoke coming out of the chimney but none from the windows. 'That's a good sign,' I thought, 'that means that the house was not burnt and is regularly functioning.' In fact, after some hours I saw a young man arrive, sent by our father, informing us that we should return to the house without fear because in the morning, with the arms and documents that he seized, he had gone to the German encampment in Itri.

Here, being completely honest, he found the treatment for the German officials to be very hospitable. He was treated for his wounds and contusions and was given bread and marmalade.

They took back the documents and weapons and apologized for the regrettable events that had happened, according to them due to a couple of black sheep and assured him that the soldiers would no longer be permitted to go about at night.

In the afternoon of November 13, 1943, or a few days after, I can't remember, we arrived at our house, still at Monticelle a German official accompanied by an armed military guard, the second in a special way, with an air of benevolence. They declared themselves to be the commander of the encampment and interpreter, and they said that they had been informed of the incident. It was explained to the interpreter who translated it in detail to the official; these two concluded that the two soldiers would be severely punished by a military tribunal, "because they were disarmed by Italians, judged to be soldiers by few." That provoked anger from my father, who had been a major in the Italian military, but the interpreter with a sense of balance and generosity did not relay these words to the commander in order to preserve the peace. Ties with the interpreter Giorgio and after.

In the days that followed, the interpreter returned often and established current fondness between us and him. He told us to call him Giorgio, and he was very polite and tactful; he very much enjoyed the local products of the family: artichokes in oil, smoked olives, baked carobs, etc.

After a few months, he suddenly disappeared together with his combat unit. The front was always moving closer, a reason for which permanence in the zone became more dangerous, especially due to the event of which I spoke.

For this reason, the family was forced to divide up: my mother and sisters went with the writer (me), and brothers Peppino and Enrico remained at the house. Here via the interpreter Giorgio, the three of them, during the unfolding of the military trial, in retaliation was taken and used for various manual labors that were necessary due to the war.

Giorgio-Fra Antimo.

Months and months passed, and Giorgio was only a dear memory for the entire family. The war ended and the remains of our beautiful house in Itri, little by little, we're able to accommodate those who were able to return. The number was intact with the help of God.

In one of the days immediately following the end of the war, following dinner, my parents saw a monk of good height and well colored arrive at the door. Asking permission to enter, he presented himself to my parents saying, "Don't you recognize me? I am Giorgio, the interpreter of that night with the Germans, 'fra Antimo' at the Franciscan monastery in Grottaferrata."

Our relationship with fra Antimo after the war was very strong, not dissimilar to that which we had during the height of the war. At the harvesting of olives, he came to stay with us in order to help and called my mother "mama Cardi."

Suddenly he was called back to Germany in order to help his elderly father, and he went to live at the Franciscan convent of Bal Tolz. It is here that he presented himself to the notary Bengl to give the present declaration that he courteously sent to us. The last correspondence from Giorgio that I have in my possession is from March 21, 1973, and at the present time, I do not know if he is still living, or if his beautiful soul is watching us from heaven.

To complete the story of the terrible night described before, I want to mention that near the end of the skirmish, Antonio Pelliccia, attracted by the screams, helped us. Also, like us, he was unarmed, now dead and who at the time lived on the top floor of the little house.

Latina, June 10, 1976

In faith, Mario Cardi

Zia Loreta and Zio Teodore Cardi family photos

Saint Pope John Paul II with Dr. Ettore Cardi

Prof. Mario Cardi and son Prof. Teodore (L)
visit to Rhode Island, attending a reception in their honor.
Stephen Cardi and Donald Migliori (R) Reception given by Domenico
Cardi family

Enrico and Tina Cardi receiving the keys to The City of Cranston, by
Mayor James Taft

Dr. Ettore Cardi and Rosalba Belfiori Studying our ancestral history, Rome, Italy

Giuseppe (Peppino) Cardi

The Domenico Cardi family and guests at Mary and Nino Barone's home for a dinner in honor of Mario, Rosaria and Teodoro Cardi

Giuseppe (Peppino) Cardi's family: Alfredo, Olinda Manzi, Lidia, Ascanio (Itri) Photo: Lidia Cardi

Vera Cardi, her husband, and son

*Cardi sisters and brothers: Americo, Anna, Gaetanina, Angolina,
Maria Civitina, and Alfred*

"Now will I praise these godly men, our ancestors, each in his own time: Some of them have left behind a name and men recount their praiseworthy deeds. At gatherings, their wisdom is retold, and the assembly proclaims their glory."

Sirach 44, VS:1-8-15 (New American Bible)

CHAPTER 23
AN APPOINTED TIME

Dedicated to all those who have passed in our lifetime and the many who have gone before us…

Each of us has an appointed time and date when we will be called home. Only God knows the time. Sometimes, it comes too soon in one's life, as with our spouses, children, mothers, fathers, grandparents, aunts, uncles, cousins, and other relatives.

My first experience of death was when our step-grandmother Maria Battista passed. She was laid out on the second-floor apartment of her home at 1707 Cranston Street (Knightsville), where she lived. Anna Migliori Ferri and I were five years old. Our aunts and Mama kept vigil around the clock. Aunt Mary Longo was not left alone. This event was impressive and scary to me as a child. The house and the surroundings looked dark, dingy, and morbid. It seemed as if we were encompassed by darkness.

Adults wore black for a year to respect the passing of their loved ones. They didn't play music, listen to the radio, and if they had a television (we didn't have a TV then), watching it was not allowed. Even though our mothers explained why we had restrictions, children had a difficult time understanding this custom.

When many of our family members and close friends passed throughout the years, relatives made sure the family had enough food. Meals were cooked daily, and our mothers would serve the grieving family. All of the aunts worked together to help out. Many close-knit cousins and friends also contributed in any way they could. That was their tradition. This custom was a great help to the families.

Mama insisted we continue this tradition throughout our lives. My sisters and I have made and brought food and dinners many times to families, and close friends who had a tragedy in their family. We still honor this custom.

I always admired my husband, Ralph, who would willingly help me deliver full-course dinners to relatives and friends. He respected my family's custom to always be charitable when people needed it, and to bring comfort and support to them.

It is hard trying to offer support to one who has lost a loved one. Attempting to offer counsel is oftentimes shallow and indifferent, unless one has walked in that person's shoes, and has personally experienced their pain and total emptiness. Nothing seems to touch the pain, the deep emotions of aloneness, and loneliness. Nothing seems to penetrate the deep void one feels after the loss of a loved one.

Each person's passage is different. One must heal in their time, and work through the various stages of grief. There is no set time frame, and individuals do not experience grief in the same way. Our lives are unique, as well as our relationships. Most people think their grief is greater than another's. We can never judge someone's grief or demand they get over it now. Silence is golden at times. A person may feel greater support when little is said. Just being there, and offering one your hand, says it all.

When Ralph and I began to lose our friends and family members, it was difficult for the spouses left behind to find their place socially. Ralph would tell me each weekend, "Get the lonely-hearts club together, we will go out to dinner." Luke had recently lost Rita and was devastated. Dodo, and other lifelong friends, plus Luke, Ralph, and I would go out to dinner. After dinner, we would go to my home or Dodo's home for dessert and coffee. This comradery each week, brought much comfort and hope to those who were lost in their loneliness, and facing life without their spouse.

I thank God for giving us so many wonderful, loving friends and relatives who have touched our lives, and for giving us a rich, meaningful heritage.

Gaetanina (Mama) with her children, grandchildren, and great-grandchildren. Celebrating her 90th birthday at Raphael's Bar-Risto

CHAPTER 24
My Prayer for You

A t times, we think that the events of the past are only treasured by us alone. Writing this book, and while talking with friends from our childhood, we were easily led back to the memories of our childhood activities while living in Cardi's yard. Who would ever think that a pear tree would be so precious to many of us? The years we spent under that pear tree and sharing our lives are unforgettable. I realize that memories are forever.

Following is an abridged inner healing prayer that I have written, asking Jesus to heal the hurts, unforgiveness, trauma, and all that has been passed down to you by your parents, family members, associates, and ancestors. I have prayed for thousands of people over the years, at large conferences, while giving retreats, or privately with church leaders, the laity, and religious.

Meditate on this prayer often and try to picture Jesus holding you in His arms as each person and situation, no matter how difficult it may be, comes to your memory. Ask Jesus for the graces you need to let go of all that is holding you in bondage, and to forgive those who have hurt you. Much will be revealed to you.

I also like and pray the novena for inner healing to Our Lady Undoer of Knots.

Heavenly Father, You, have shown me love and mercy throughout my life, through Your Son Jesus Christ. I praise and thank You for all You have given to me, and desire to praise You forever. I consider the love with which You suffered and died for me, and the radiant joy with which You rose from the dead.

Yet, Father, I dare to ask You for even more, through the intercession of the Immaculate Conception of the Blessed Virgin Mary, and Our Lord and Savior Jesus Christ. We know You, and I, that I am wounded. In my sins and the sins of others, the reality of evil and harm has touched me. Lord, I ask that you heal me of these wounds. Cleanse my parental, and ancestral bloodline of all the effects and trauma's that were passed on to me, at the moment of my conception.

You healed the lepers, the lame, those who were barren, and those who were tormented by demons. You raised the dead, healed those who feared to step forward, and those who were steeped in self-pity and self-hatred. You showed compassion to sinners and welcomed those who betrayed, rejected, condemned, and abandoned You.

I ask for the grace to love all the individuals who have abused and hurt me; that made me feel abandoned, rejected, misunderstood, worthless and condemned. Heal me of the indifference I felt from them, and all that has caused me to sin towards them and You.

I hold each person up to you Lord and ask for Your blessing upon them. Give me the graces I need to love my enemies, as You love them, and to forgive them as You forgive them.

Give me the gift of Your unconditional love, which destroys the resentments, hurts, and trauma's in my life.

Examples of what to pray for in your ancestral and personal history:

To be healed of the hurts and trauma's that you have experienced e.g. incest, rape, mental and physical abuse, bullying, self-hatred, abandonment, poverty, addictions to sex, alcohol, and drugs. Cancers: brain, bladder, kidney, leukemia, blood disorders, non-Hodgkin's lymphoma, multiple myeloma, breast, lung, pancreatic, liver, bone, muscular, melanoma, throat, stomach, esophagus, colon, and auto-immune disorders. Mental illnesses: schizophrenia, bipolar, social anxiety disorder, depression, ADHD, and self-destruction. Crippling accidents e.g. paralyzing injuries, suffocation, drowning, homicide, suicide. Dishonesty and greed (taking someone else's goods or money). Illnesses: cardiovascular disease, dementia, Alzheimer's, eating disorders, retardation. Abnormal births, abortions, miscarriages, adultery, satanic practices, and curses. Worshipping false gods, pagan worship, and unbelief.

Add what applies to you if it is not listed…

Heal me and my family from the very beginning of time. Heal me of all traumas I experienced while in my mother's womb, during my birth, and throughout my life.

Bring peace, unity, health, and love to me and my family, and all future generations. Heal all those who no longer believe in You, the one true God. Lord, break the bond of evil acts in my ancestral bloodline that still touches my life. Bridge the gap in the love You have for me, and the love I experience from others.

Lord, I give all to you. I praise and thank you for calling me by name. Give me the grace to know what You have called me to do in my life, and the graces to fulfill your plan for me.

I hold my family members and future generations up to you, that the evils of others will not touch their lives. I ask for Your blessings upon them, and all that they are called to accomplish. Open the right doors for them and bless their professions, livelihood, marriages, children, and offspring to the end of time. May Your light and love shine through each of us to bring Your healing love to all those we encounter.

I give You the honor and praise forever and thank You for all You have done for me. With Your precious blood, purify my bloodline and DNA from the beginning of time.

Madonna della Civita, and Our Lady of Lourdes, pray for me and mine.

Oh! Mary conceived without sin, pray for me who have recourse to You. I ask you to place your mantle of protection over me and my family.

Our Lady Undoer of the Knots set me and my family free from all of the bondage in our lives, that have been passed down to us by our parents and ancestors.

St. Joseph, place your cloak over me and my family. Amen.

Believe in yourself. I love each of you.

Forever with love,
Mom, Nonni, Daudi, Sister, Auntie Bert, Bern, Cousin,
In order to continue our story, add your history and please,

Capotosto, Conte, Geaudreau, Izzo, Ostrowski, Vartanian, Giannini

Leo Matthew Murphy, Jr.

CAPOTOSTOS FROM AUSTRALIA, ITRI AND NEW YORK

Angela Cardillo, Onorato, wife (R) and Debbie Agresti.
Capotosto family from Australia

Capotosto Uncles
Luigino Sinapi, Nonno Onorato, Papa, Zio Vincenzo, Costanzo

Vincenzo Capotosto family
Zio Vincenzo, Amalia, Nicolina Dante, Sergio, Ilda (Itri)

Orlando and son

*Lorraine, Robert, Albert, Bernadette, Bessie, Anna Izzo, Danny Jr., Aunt
Angelina Fusco*

Bob Fusco, Cosmo, and Ed Fusco (N.Y.)

Zio Vincenzo Capotosto with Capotostos at Conte home

Cousin Lotti Sinapi, Bernadette, Anna, and Marie

Ralph Conte and Frank Sinapi from NY

Mama, Aldo, Zio Vincenzo at Conte home
His visit to America

Luke and Capotosto cousins rebuilding a bridge in Itri destroyed in WWII

Luke on one of Nonno Onorato's fruit trees, Itri

Cousins Cosmo and Mary Picano Ruggieri

Cousin John Picano

CARDI RELATIVES FROM ITRI, FLORENCE, AND FONDI

Monsignor Alfredo Cardi, Son of Antonio

Don Gregorio Cardi, Son of Pasquale

Zio Alfredo Cardi, author Recorder of family history

Don Vergilio Mancini and Fr. Roland Cardi

First cousins Domenico, Fiori, and Vincenzo Cardi

Dr. Vincenzo and Alfonso Di Biase

*Vincenzo, Alfonso, Patrizia, looking at Photos and letter from
Grandpa Antonio*

Dinner at Ascanio Cardi's home, Itri, 2013
Olinda Manzi, Bernadette, Lidia, Alfonso, Ascanio, Maria Rosaria

Uncle Alfred, Paolo Di Biase, Gaetanina (Mama), Uncle Rico,
Angie Cantone at Conte home

Paola Sepe Cardi and Gianpaolo Cardi

Samuel, Deborah, Scott Ostrowski's trip to Itri, visit with Gianpaolo Cardi

Gianpaolo, Cenza Cardi, Bernadette, former Mayor Giovanni Ialongo

CONTE

Paul and Mary Conte

Maria Domenica Martini, Raffael Conti family (Mary Conti's family)

Paul, Ralph, Gloria, William, Fred, Richard Conte

Kali Melone, Briana, Lori and Katherine Conte

Kali, Raphael, Zoë, Ralph, Michael, Paul, Leland Conte

The Twins: William and Richard Conti

Mary and Fred Conti family: Fred, Debbie, Mary, Fred, Judy, Al, Briana, Shalyn, Gloria

Linda Conte Messina

Barbara and Paul Conte

Cindy, Bianca, Richard (R.J.) Conti

The Hunts: Gloria, Deborah, Linda, Gloria

Harold Hunt

Cousins: Ralph, Tony, and Bob Conte

Ralph and Katherine with Cousin Marianna in Fondi, Italy

Ralph with his Conte cousins in Fondi.
Owners of Conte fruit and produce, Fondi, Italy

CARDI

Aunt Jeanette Cardi

Stephen, Robert, Stephanie La Tour, Maria Kadison, and
Mariana La Tour

Stephen, Alfred, Marianna, Antonio, Maria Cardi

Antonio and Els Cardi

Will and Maria Kadison

Caroline and David Gardy family
Daughters: Sarah and Celeste

Stephen and Noel Cardi

Rose and Stephen Cardi

Stephen Cardi

Annie and Nico Mc Gough

Aunt Alene, and Maria Cardi

Louise and Alfred, Aunt Alene, Maria, Marianna, Alfred, Pamela Cardi

Christopher Cardi

Alphonse B. Cardi

Jeanette, Anthony, Buddy, Donna, Paula, Felicita Cardi

Anthony P. and Marian Cardi family

Anthony P. Cardi and Cosmo Capotosto

CRUDALE

Aunt Angie and Uncle Arthur Crudale family with sons and their families: Angelo, wife Etta, Arthur wife Rose, Alphonse wife Pat and families

Patricia and Alphonse Crudale family

Etta and Angelo Crudale family: Dr. Angelo, Audrey, Stephen

FERRI

Anna Migliori Ferri and William Ferri

The Ferri family Dr. William, Kenneth, Ray, Dr. Paul, Maryann, David, Annette

Maryann and Anthony Crudale Photos: Maryann Crudale

LONGO

Aunt Maria Civitina Cardi Longo, pharmacist

Marilyn Longo and Donna Di Michele

Maria Longo Stringer

Maria and Howard Stringer with Bernadette in England

Donna and Michael Di Michele with Rose Cardi

MIGLIORI

Gloria and Dr. Julius Migliori

The Migliori family: Drs. Richard, Mark, Julius, Stephen, Gloria, Jill, Att. Donald, Dr. Michael

Dr. Joseph Migliori

The Joanne and Att. Donald Migliori family

Drs. Sydney and Stephen Migliori

Dr. Michael and Marianna Migliori

MEMORIES

Julius Migliori, Uncle Alfred Cardi, Luke Capotosto behind the steering wheel

Aunts Angelina Crudale and Anna Migliori Under the pear tree

Uncle Joseph Migliori with friends, Uncles Alfred and Rico Cardi in front of the Medical Arts Pharmacy

ROSA AND DOMENICO CARDI FAMILY

THE FOUNDERS OF CARDI'S FURNITURE

Marian, Rosa and Nicholas

Peter Cardi

Nicholas Cardi

SONS OF MARIAN and NICHOLAS CARDI

Nicholas, Ron, and Pete

NEIGHBOR MEMORIES

Lillian Church, Angela Ialongo, Anna and Marie Capotosto with friends

Neighborhood women: Sinapi, Soprano, Capotosto, Cardi

Jeanette Palumbo with Maria Cardi and Linda Palumbo
Photo: Jeanette Palumbo D'Amico

Charlie Lepezzera, Manny Palumbo, Inside Medical Arts Pharmacy

Capotosto, Cardi, Migliori, Palumbo and Perrino children
Photo: Jeanette Palumbo D'Amico

Cardis and Palumbos
Photo: Jeanette Palumbo D'Amico

Madeline and Tom Vellucci, and Clare Mc Parlin

Victor Di Costa, Have Gun will travel, "Paladin"

Frank Sinapi, Bernadette, Frank Lepezzera Committee for the first and
only Knightsville Reunion (The Providence Journal)

Inside of Saccoccio's Drug Store

Soprano's Market

Original Cranston City Hall and Police Station Photo: Cranston Historical Society

*Narragansett Hotel, Knigtsville
Photo: Cranston Historical Society*

*De Luca's Hill
Cranston Historical Society*

APPENDIX

INHERITANCE INVENTORY

By the Grace of God and the Will of the Nation
Present KING of Italy - Vittorio Emanuele III

This year 1929 (7th year of the Fascist Era) on the 17th of June, at 9:50 AM, in the town called Itri, in the house of the registered residence of the deceased Gaetana Pernarella (daughter of Luigi, widow of Domenico's son Cardi Alfonso) located in Corso Vittorio Emanuele II.
Abiding Court instance promoted by Mr. Ascanio Teodoro Cardi (son of Antonio), a resident teacher in Itri, in his official role of representative of the general heirs Domenico and Vincenzo Cardi (sons of Alfonso and Gaetana Pernarella). See also separate proxy acts stipulated in Providence, United States of America, by the notary Pietro Antonio Russo, on the 7th of December,1928, registered also in Fondi (Italy) on the 27th of March,1929, Doc. No. 269, again registered today as attachment Ref. 27.

I, Onofrio Pennacchia (son of Mattia), resident notary public in Itri, enrolled on the Collegial List of Notaries, district of Rome and Velletri, as an appointee of the bailiff of Fondi district (see attachment A - dated April 25 current year). I am here in charge of removing the seals of this house in order to proceed with an inventory of all objects, furniture, and possessions that belonged to GAETANA PERNARELLA (daughter of Luigi).

Participants and witnesses here present are:

CARDI ASCANIO TEODORO (son of Antonio), profession teacher, resident in Itri, domiciled in Corso Appio Claudio. Promotor of the instance and official guardian of the seals and goods in the house (see assembly minutes on the 9th of November 1928).
CAPOBIANCO ERASMO (son of Pasquale), profession chugger, resident and domiciled in Gaeta, in Piazza Cavallo.
Official representative of Gaetana Pernarella's son and legitimate heir.

ANTONIO CARDI (son of Alfonso), profession landowner, domiciled in Itri, resident in the United States (see legalized certification by Achille G. Verdena Notary Public of Providence, 31st of October 1928).

CARDI IMMACOLATA, daughter and legitimate heir of GAETANA PERNARELLA, profession housewife, resident in Itri, domiciled in Vicolo Giudea.

Francesco de Pinto (son of Mariano), profession town barber in Itri, assists me in the acquisition of the summons (attachment B) of Cardi Immacolata (assisted by her lawyer PAOLO D'ETTORE) and Capobianco Erasmo, both cited by the prosecutor on the 24th of May through the Bailiff GIUSEPPE BIANCHI carried out. The witnesses are eligible by law and known to us.

I have carried out the task assigned as follows:
Having read the ordinances C and D (removal of the seals affixed on the entrance), I made a visual inspection of the integrity of the seals affixed on the 9th of November 1920, since everyone assures me that there are no individual properties, I remove seals and proceed with the description and estimate value of furniture.

PECORONE PAOLO is the expert master carpenter nominated to give his professional opinion. I have exhorted him, recommending moral importance of his oath, of his religious bond contracted before God, his obligation to declare the truth and only the pure truth.

FURNITURE: First floor, the first room was reached upon climbing the staircase.
Small fir wood shelf hooked on the wall. Size 55 x 65 centimeters. The very poor condition determined the Value of 1 lira.

Small cherry wood NIGHT TABLE with a linked shelf containing a few books that everyone present acknowledged as belonging to Amedeo Rolando Cardi. Value 25 lire.

Fir wood COMMODE with walnut veneering, containing 4 pullout drawers and a marble top. A small PETTINEUS lying on top of the marble. Teodoro Cardi declares that the object is not part of the heredity because it belongs to Maria Civita Saccoccio (deceased wife of Antonio Cardi, son of Alfonso). Whereas, Immacolata Cardi disputes that the marble cover of the commode belongs to the deceased Gaetana Pernarella. Total value 130 lire.

Double-size WROUGHT IRON BED, acknowledged by all to belong to Rosina Corpolongo, wife of Cardi Domenico. Value 40 lire.

Iron BABY CRIB. Value 15 lire.
Small fir wood TABLE. Value 20 lire.

A military wooden (fir wood) CRATE. Everyone present agrees that it belongs to Rosina Corpolongo. Value 18 lire.

A wooden COMMODE (VENEERED WALNUT), with 4 pullout drawers, and a marble top. Two glass bells are placed on the marble top. One contains the image of the Immaculate Conception; the second bell contains artificial flowers. Standing close to the glass bells there is one small statue of Saint Joseph and 3 tiny flower vases. With the exception of the last 2 items, all the rest belongs to Rosina Corpolongo, as everyone acknowledges and agrees. Value 18 lire.

Wrought iron INFANT BED with a metallic base. Value 45 lire

Wrought iron FULL-SIZE BED. Value 25 lire
An empty walnut CRATE that everyone agrees belonging to the deceased Maria Civita Saccoccio. Value 30 lire.

Old BARBER CHAIR that everyone acknowledges belonging to Cardi Vincenzo. Value 15 lire.
Three STRAW MATTRESSES: (2 vegetable mats and 1 animal feather mat).

Four PILLOWS: (3 feathers and 1 wool). Total value 10 lire.
Three small fir wood TABLES. Total value 8 lire.

Seventeen STRAW CHAIRS: (Only 5 in fair condition). Total value 30 lire.

Old PENDULUM CLOCK. Value 50 lire.
Fifteen small MINIATURE PICTURES showing knights on horses. Value 3 lire.

Small WALL HANGER with 3 knobs and 2 white metal cross hooks. Value 5 lire.
Two old COPPER BOILERS (LARGE AND SMALL),

FOUR copper pans, one COPPER PAN COVER, (all these items heavily used and consumed).
One broken BRAZIER.
One very old CEDAR COPPER BASIN
One TINY DEEP white iron pan
One tin COLANDER

One WHITE IRON POT One ENAMELED IRON POT One WHITE IRON CASSEROLE

One small WHITE ENAMELED BROTH DRAINER

Four TIN PAN COVERS

One ENAMELED IRON TUG

One very small ENAMELED IRON TUG

One IRON FRYING PAN and one IRON GRILL

One bottomless TIN MEASURING CUP

One BRASS AND STONE SCALE (Cardi Immacolata sustains that it belonged to her father. Meanwhile, Cardi Teodoro sustains it belonged to Vincenzo Cardi.

Two old fir wood CUPBOARDS.

A TIN CUP (probably a remaining piece of a hand scale that no longer exists).

An old enameled iron BASIN.

A plaster MONEY JAR.

A small fake FRUIT BASKET made of chalk.

A small PLASTER DOG.

A small PLASTER PARROT.

A small PLASTER DOLL.

Two small HORNS made of PLASTER.

Three COFFEE CUPS with three bottom COFFEE PLATES.

A broken GLASS VASE.

These ten objects are in a very worn-out condition.

Total value 50 lire.

At this point in the inventory, everyone present requires to suspending the activity and postpone the continuation of the inventory. As a notary public, I agree to a postponement of the remaining inventory. The continuation will begin on Thursday, 20th of this current month, at 10 AM. All present intervened to come punctually without any further notice. The draft of this first inventory act has been drawn up under the continuous supervision of all the witnesses and experts who will each sign the draft at the end and also on the side of each page.

I have personally dictated the compilation of this document consisting of three sheets, 10 side facades, and attachments A, B, C, D.

I, the notary, have read the inventory papers completed until today with everyone present, with a loud and clear voice. All the participants have declared that the script complies with their truth of the site inspection.

The witnesses have declared that the content complies with their will and their truth.

All participants sign the inventory papers at 10, 20.
Cardi, Ascanio Teodoro
Capobianco, Erasmo
Cardi, Immacolata

Paolo D'Ettore (Lawyer)
Pecorone, Paolo (Expert)
De Pinto, Francesco (witness)
De Rocco, Luigi (wi
Onofrio Pennacchia (Notary Public)

CONTINUATION OF INHERITANCE INVENTORY
By the Grace of God and the Will of the Nation
Present King of Italy - Vittorio Emanuele III
This year 1929 (7th year of the Fascist Era), on the 20th of June, at 10:15 AM, in the town of ITRI, in the house as registered residence of the deceased GAETANA PERNARELLA (DAUGHTER OF LUIGI, WIDOW OF CARDI ALFONSO), located in CORSO VITTORIO EMANUELE II.

I, ONOFRIO PENNACCHIA (son of Mattia), resident Notary Public in ITRI, enrolled on the Collegial List of Notaries, district of Rome and Velletri, in accordance with what is stated in the minutes drawn up on the 17th of the present month and in the presence of the same suitable participants with the exception of Lawyer Paolo D'Ettore who did not attend, and with the addition of Ascanio Teodoro Cardi's lawyer, Manzi Francesco, I am continuing the inventory as follows:

We opened the drawers of the 2 COMMODES standing in the first room where the inventory started. In one commode we find:

2 pieces of REDLINING FABRIC (often used to cover one side of bed blankets).
1 WOOL SWEATER
4 PHOTOS

In the second commode we find:
A small CARTON BOX containing GOLD OBJECTS and 1 KEY. Appraisal of gold value is entrusted to the nominated PETRILLO ERNESTO DI GIOVANNI, a jeweler. He has been given my admonition regarding the moral significance of his oath, a religious bond in front of God, obligations to declare truth faithfully with the purpose of making known a pure truth.

GOLD OBJECTS FOUND ARE:

1. STRING of gold weighing 17 grams. Value lire 130.
2. CORNEY RING, a pair of EARRINGS, one PENDANT, THIN BAND RING, THIN RING LOOP, all used. Total gold weight 11.50 grams. Total value lire 40.
All of the above-found gold items have been valued by the same one jeweler for the total value of lire 32 and 50 cents.
An ENEMA was also found in the drawer, Value lire 8.
Now, both the expert jeweler and lawyer Manzi have left the room.

There is nothing else, so we also leave this room and proceed to the next. Master carpenter Pecoraro Paolo (son of Achille) is given my admonition regarding the moral significance of his oath, religious bond in front of God, obligation to declare truth faithfully with the purpose of making known the pure truth. He will give his expert opinion on the following objects:

3. One old WALNUT STANDOFF with marble top, Capobianco Erasmo declares it belongs to Rosina Corpolongo. Cardi Immacolata disagrees and contradicts him. Value lire 15.

4. One old double WROUGHT IRON BED. Fir boards on base. Value lire 70.

5. One old MATTRESS made of straw mixed with cloth, 2 WOOL MATTRESSES, and QUILT BLANKET, 2 vegetable PILLOWS, 1 WOOL PILLOW, 1 FEATHER PILLOW, 4 PILLOW COVERS, 1 TABLECLOTH, 1 SMALL TOWEL, 1 SMALL TABLECLOTH, 1 COTTON-WOOL BED COVER (threadbare), 3 VERY WORN-OUT SHEETS (one has a lace edge). Total value lire 200.

6. One old COMMODE (walnut finishing), no marble top, and 3 drawers containing EMPTY MEDICINE BOXES in the first drawer, 5 used PERCALE SHIRTS, 2 old jersey SHIRTS, 1 petticoat, ONE old underpants, 1 handkerchief, one piece of MEDICATION BANDAGE in the second drawer. 2 old jersey SHIRTS, 1 OLD PETTICOAT, 1 old UNDERPANTS, 1 HANDKERCHIEF, one piece of MEDICATION BANDAGE in the second drawer, 2 OLD MALE SHIRTS, 1 BATHING SUIT, 1 PILLOW COVER, 2 glass bells containing a plaster baby Jesus in one and a plaster Madonna in the other. A hand mirror was on top of all the items contained in the third drawer, Erasmo Capobianco declares the mirror to belong to Vincenzo Cardi. Immacolata Cardi contradicts. Total value lire 105.

7. One old and rickety PETTINEUS, veneered with fir wood, with marble top. Everyone acknowledges belonging to Rosina Corpolongo. Value lire 8.

8. Enameled wrought iron BASIN in its holder. Value lire 2 and 50 cents.

9. Twenty clay DISHES, 1 enameled iron DISH (all old). 15 WINE GLASSES, 9 LIQUOR GLASSES, 6 GLASS JUGS, 2 GLASS FRUIT BOWLS, 2 GLASS WATER BOTTLES, 2 very old TIN GLOVES, 1 CLAY MUG, 2 CLAY BOWLS, 5 COFFEE CUPS

and 6 UNDER PLATES, 2 OIL LIGHTS, 1 small enameled PAN, 1 enameled IRON FUNNEL, 2 enameled IRON COFFEE VESSELS, 1 SPIRIT LAMP, 3 CLAY SALAD BOWLS, 5 empty BOTTLES, 7 empty MEDICINE BOTTLE, 2 empty LIQUOR BOTTLES, 17 worn out TIN SPOONS, 4 TIN FORKS, 4 GERMAN SILVER FORKS, 3 TIN COFFEE SPOONS, 1 GERMAN SILVER SMALL SPOON, FLOUR STAPLE made with wire. 1 old TOMATO TIN PRESS, 7 different sizes COPPER BAKE PANS, 1 CASSEROLE WITH LID, 1 SMALLER CASSEROLE, 1 BRASS COLANDER, 1 BRASS PAN, 1 small white cloth covering a niche in the wall. Total value lire 120.

10. 22 SMALL PICTURES hanging on the wall. 5 are figures of horse jockeys, 17 are photos.

1 WALL HANGER with 3 poplar wood knobs.

5 straw CHAIRS.

Total value lire 55.

11. Old poplar TRUNK containing a kilo of dried almonds, 1 hammer, various papers, letters, postcards, receipts of paid taxes, other various certificates that do not in any way pertain to the present heredity, and a 25 lire STOCK CERTIFICATE of Cooperative Bank of Fondi belonging to Cardi Alfonso (son of Domenico) which I, as notary, take official note of.

 Noticing the late hour, everyone requires suspension of the inventory until the next day.

As a notary public, I agree with the postponement. The inventory will continue tomorrow, Friday, at 6 AM. Everyone is recalled being punctually present.

The draft of this second inventory has been drawn up under the continuous supervision of all the witnesses and experts who will each sign the draft at the end and along the sides of each page.

I personally dictated the compilation of this second inventory consisting of 3 sheets handwritten by a trusted person under my supervision.

The draft of this second inventory has been drawn up under the continuous supervision of all the witnesses and experts who will each sign the end page and along the sides of each page.

I have personally dictated the compilation of this document consisting of 3 sheets written by a trustworthy person.
I have read the script with a loud and clear voice to all the participants that declare that the contents comply with the truth of the inspection.

All signed at 13 hours and 30 minutes (1 PM).
Cardi, Ascanio Teodoro
Capobianco, Erasmo
Cardi, Immacolata
Pecorone, Paolo (expert)
De Pinto, Francesco (witness)
De Rocco, Luigi
Onofrio Pennacchia (Notary)

CONTINUATION INHERITANCE INVENTORY

By the Grace of God and the Will of the Nation
Present King of Italy - Vittorio Emanuele III
This year 1929 (7th year of the Fascist Era), on the 21st of June, at 6:30 AM, in the house of the registered residence of the deceased GAETANA PERNARELLA (daughter of Luigi) and widow of CARDI ALFONSO, situated in Corso Vittorio Emanuele in Itri, I (Onofrio Pennacchia, son of Mattia and Notary Public in Itri) will continue the inventory as indicated in the document drawn up yesterday.

All yesterday's participants are present, with the exception of Capobianco Erasmo (son of Pasquale). Also present is Francesco De Pinto (son of Mariano who is a barber in Itri). Also present is De Rocco Luigi (son of Giorgio) born in Naples and retired in Itri. These last two are suitable witnesses and legally acknowledged by all.

Lawyer Manzi Francesco is present on behalf of Ascanio Teodoro Cardi.

Nothing more to inspect in the second room, we will walk on to the attic area which is on the same floor level (first floor). It consists of a small area used as a storage closet. For this purpose, I require the professional evaluation of master carpenter Pecorone Paolo (son of Achille) who swears to say the pure truth.

The objects found are the following:

Three TIN PITCHERS (one is bigger than the other two), coated on the inside to store
oil, wine, or grains.

Two old chestnut BUCKETS used for grapes. One tiny firewood SHELF hung on wall.

Two big empty GLASS BOTTLES (1.5 liters and 5 liters and 5 liters capacity).

Two old iron DECILITERS (measuring cup for liquids).

One EARTHENWARE deep CONED PAN.

One CRETE AMPHORA.

One iron HEAVER

One pair of OLD BOOTS.

One HOE.

One old and broken piece of HORSE FILAMENT.

One old wooden ladder.

One broken piece of CHAIN probably belonging to
a barrow.

Three CLOTH BAGS.

Three SCREW AUGERS.

One FILE.

One set of PLIERS (tongs).

One COMPASS.

One portion of an IRON BEAM.

All the listed above are old and worn, total value lire 50.

In the same location we also found:

Two HORSE SADDLE STRUCTURES. Two CRATES.

One WOODEN WINC. Two fir wood WAGON SEATS.
One SMALL chestnut wood WINDOW. One old BRASS BASIN.
One 6.20 meters long CHESTNUT BEAM.
Two and a half chestnut BOARDS.
One old and broken BUCKSAW.
Seven CLAY POTS for flowers.
Approximately 2 quintals of SWAMP HAY.
Two sitting BOARDS (for the wagon) that Cardi
Immacolata claims to be her exclusive property.
Ascanio Teodoro Cardi confirms the truth of the claim.
One FIR BOARD Total value lire 200

Nothing else is in the attic storage, we directed down to the ground space surrounding the entrance to the house.

Capobianco Erasmo takes note of all has been inspected at this point. I officially asked Cardi Immacolata, Cardi Ascanio Teodoro, and Capobianco Erasmo, on their own honor, if they know of anything else that we should inspect or if they acknowledge any missing items, goods, or possessions.

Cardi Immacolata declared that, to her knowledge, there is nothing else to be checked. She also declared that she is not in a position to know if there are missing items.

Conversely, Ascanio Teodoro Cardi declares that there are missing 3 geese, 1 hen, 2 blankets (light blue and white), 2 wool jerseys, 1 silk suit, sheets, pillow covers, towels, sweaters, woolen shirts, a pair of shoes, and general house linens that Cardi Immacolata has taken to her house.

Capobianco Erasmo declares that he has no knowledge of additional possessions nor of missing items.

Cardi Immacolata explains that after her mother's death, she was entrusted the animals' welfare - grazing, guarding, and feeding the 3 geese and one hen. Cardi Immacolata furthermore explains that she was entrusted with various other articles such as shirts, silk suits, blankets, sheets, as well as a dirty sweater belonging to Amedeo Cardi that she had washed, a pair of shoes, and other items that are all detailed and listed in a private written agreement she signed with Antonio Cardi. So since then, she has always been ready to return all listed goods.

All papers, objects, and furniture, including gold objects and the 25 lire stock certificate, are delivered to the nominated trustee, Mr. Francesco De Pinto (son of Mariano, town barber), resident in Itri.

Inventory finishes now, I have personally directed the compilation of the document consisting of sheets handwritten by a person we trust. I will read the text of the document with a loud and clear voice so that everyone can approve it, and if compliant with the facts they will all sign on the final sheet, and on the margin of the first sheet. Time of signature 9:10 AM.

Ascanio Teodoro Cardi
Capobianco, Erasmo
Cardi, Immacolata
Pecorone, Paolo (expert)
Francesco Manzi (lawyer)
De Pinto, Francesco (witness)
De Rocco, Luigi (witness)
Onofrio Pennacchia (notary)
ITRI, July 7th, 1929

De Rocco Luigi receives from Notary Onofrio Pennacchia the amount of 15 lire for the tribute as a witness during the three sessions of the inventory at Pernarella's house.

CARDI INVENTORY

Note of expenses and fees:

Appeal (papers and fees)

.... 17,00

Copy.. 5,10

Copy of the minutes and

seals.. .8,10

Summons.. 41,25

Notary... 50,00

Inventory... 95,50

Inventory... 79,50

Inventory... 76,50

Registration tax.. 50,30

TOTAL:.. 423,25

Expert Witness

Luigi.. 15,000

Expert Pecoraro....................................... 45,000

Witness De Pinto...................................... 20,000

Total: 503,250

Made in United States
North Haven, CT
19 October 2021

10423281R00144